Reflections

Comments on 'The Seven Valleys'

REFLECTIONS

Comments on

'The Seven Valleys'

of

Bahá'u'lláh

By

Jenabe E. Caldwell

Best Publisher
Wailuku, Hawaii
http://www.jenabe.org

Reflections

Published by Best Publisher
Wailuku, Hawaii

http://www.jenabe.net

©Jenabe E. Caldwell
All rights reserved

Second Edition 2008

ISBN: 0-9762780-5-7

Contents

Foreword	vii
Introduction	ix
The Seven Valleys of Bahá'u'lláh	1
The Valley of Search	9
The Valley of Love	25
The Valley of Knowledge	30
The Valley of Unity	48
The Valley of Contentment	73
The Valley of Wonderment	76
The Valley of True Poverty and Absolute Nothingness	84

Foreword

In *Reflections*, Caldwell takes his readers on a written journey that is the fruit of his many years of service to the Cause of Bahá'u'lláh. Throughout the Bahá'í world, this Knight of Bahá'u'lláh has assisted countless friends in the process of spiritual transformation as the facilitator of "Nine-Day Institutes" during which time participants are submerged in deep study of *The Seven Valleys* as well as other Sacred Writings. Caldwell's ability to carefully listen to the insights of the hundreds of friends who have participated in such institutes as well as his own experiences in teaching and serving the Cause of Bahá'u'lláh have given fruition in *Reflections* in which he synthesizes and summarizes the salient features of this poetic and often mysterious Book. Written in plain language, people of all ages and backgrounds will enjoy and understand the simple truths that Caldwell has uncovered. Caldwell's gift for storytelling is especially effective in making clear important principles such as reliance on God, patience, resignation and love.

Whether individually or in study groups, readers of *Reflections* may discover that they are more able to effectively understand *The Seven Valleys* if they consider and examine their own lives and daily experiences in service to the Cause. By following the process of "reflection" as exemplified in Caldwell's book, it is hoped that readers may gain an appreciation for the dynamic and real-life value that *The Seven Valleys* and other Sacred Scriptures have in assisting them in the process of spiritual transformation. Although their own cultures and life experiences may dramatically differ from those presented in Caldwell's book, readers will hopefully discover that the spiritual and moral principles enshrined in Bahá'u'lláh's Words are in operation throughout the lives of each and every individual as they make their journey through the valleys of life.

Naomi ˋKomoda

Introduction

"The Seven Valleys" was written to a Sufi Mystic in answer to his questions. This Book was one of the first Books revealed by Bahá'u'lláh who during His lifetime revealed hundreds of Books and Tablets. The questions asked seem to be about death in God and life through Him, and about love for the beloved of God and His Manifestations.

Let me make it clear at the very beginning that no human mind or pen can even begin to understand or comment in a befitting way on these Writings of Bahá'u'lláh. As I readily admit to my lack of ability and capacity you can understand that my comments are those of a finite human being reflecting on the infinite.

As a part of this introduction we will have to agree on God and the Manifestation of God. God is single, alone and unknowable. No mind can comprehend or know Him. Being unknowable we would waste time in pretending that we know Him, even in a most infinitesimal way.

Let us imagine a most tremendous power house that is generating enormous amounts of power. The power then flows through the power lines to the area of our house. We have in the house a light socket and in the socket is a light bulb. I turn on the switch and the light comes on. First, the power must be transformed down to a usable level. Then it must be fed into my house and I must have a good light bulb and even with all that I must make the effort to get the light by turning on the switch. This power house we will call God and the Holy Spirit is like the current. The transformer and light bulb is like the Manifestation of God. I am not a transformer nor am I a light bulb, and if I try to be and put myself in the socket all I will do is get electrocuted. These great Teachers are created to be our light source. Created as light bulbs it was the light of Enoch, at another time the light of Moses, then Krishna, then Buddha, Zoroaster, then Christ. At a later time it was Muhammad. Then in 1844 it was His Holiness the Báb, and for today, our source of light is Bahá'u'lláh. Now if I am a lover of light, I will love the light from whatever source it comes from. If I am only a lover of the light bulb, then, even if the light goes out and I am in total darkness I still cling to my old worn out and used up light bulb.

Because these Manifestations are directly connected to the Source, God, what They say and what They write and what They do is a Mirror of what God says, writes and does. The fundamental teachings of each of these great Teachers are the same and only differ in the needs of the students at the times of Their revelations. These teachings of God are progressive, and mankind's need for light must also evolve along with man. What we need today is much different than what was required in the days of Buddha or Christ.

Of course we have many theories about creation. The "Big Bang" is one of them. Now the big question about the big bang is what banged, and where did it come from? One of the teachings of Bahá'u'lláh is that science and religion must agree. If science does not agree with the truth of religion then it is a man-made theory. On the other hand, if religion does not agree with the truth of science then religion is only superstition.

Some say that creation was accidental. Again, by way of analogy, let us consider a printing factory that has all the letters needed to make a big unabridged dictionary from "A" to "Z". Now let's take a simple blade of grass, and not even consider the most important part of that blade of grass which is life. When we take it apart element by element, atom by atom, molecule by molecule from the purely scientific view it is as impossible to have been made by accident as it would be if we had an explosion in our printing factory and ended up with a big unabridged dictionary formed by the falling letters after the explosion with no errors.

Any reasonable man must readily agree to the fact that as a picture needs a painter, so a creation needs a Creator. Call it force, call it power, call it primal energy or for a better word call it God. Whatever we can think of is limited by our being a part of finite creation. When we say God is Love, we limit God because God is the Creator of love. This puts it beyond explanation. In the Seven Valleys we can solve the mystery of life, of the soul and spirit and become aware that the valleys we go through bring us nearer to our Creator through the aid of His Manifestation.

This Seven Valleys can be read as any other book and from the reading the spirit of man can be lifted up. However, to study and meditate on these seven steps can transform that human spirit into a heavenly light that would illuminate his life, and future generations.

THE SEVEN VALLEYS OF BAHÁ'U'LLÁH

In the Name of God, the Clement, the Merciful

Praise be to God Who hath made being to come forth from nothingness; graven upon the Tablet of man the secrets of preexistence; taught him from the mysteries of divine utterance that which he knew not; made him a Luminous Book unto those who believed and surrendered themselves; caused him to witness the creation of all things (Kullu Shay') in this black and ruinous age, and to speak forth from the apex of eternity with a wondrous voice in the Excellent Temple: to the end that every man may testify, in himself, by himself, in the station of the Manifestation of his Lord, that verily there is no God save Him, and that every man may thereby win his way to the summit of realities, until none shall contemplate anything whatsoever but that he shall see God therein.

In this passage at the very beginning of *The Seven Valleys*, we are told something of the power of God. Only a supreme intelligence, power and force could take nothing and create this creation. At one time it was thought that the atom was the smallest indivisible particle. However, our science of today has gone into the atom, and what we have found is a tremendous force and space, as we have now even broken into the nucleus of the atom we have found greater force and more nothingness.

The word graven seems to imply something that is cut deeply into man. A Tablet is something written or read. What Bahá'u'lláh seems to be saying here is that what is written and engraved deeply into man are the secrets of eternity. Preexistence is an interesting word because it implies that even before existence there was God and He has put this eternal something into man.

Many of the Holy Books have said that man was created in the image of God. Here, again, Bahá'u'lláh confirms this. The only preexistence is God, and this secret is potentially in man.

The Teachings of God come forth from the mouths of His Great Teachers. As it has come from the source of the Unknowable Essence it is indeed a deep mystery, yet He reveals these truths which we can only know through these heaven-sent Teachers. The Teachings of Bahá'u'lláh, if followed, can solve all the problems faced by our present and future civilization.

It would seem that the Luminous Book referred to in the above passage would be the Revealed Book or again the heaven-sent Teachers. The Luminous Book specifically refers to the Bayán as the translation of Bayán is "The Luminous Book". So this could mean the Báb. Here we are called upon to surrender ourselves to God's will. To surrender one's self to God seems to mean to put the Teachings of God as a top priority in our lives. This does not imply, according to the Teachings of Bahá'u'lláh, giving up job, family, friends and our calling in life. It means that one should go to the Teachings of Bahá'u'lláh for the answers on what to do with job, family, friends and living.

Kullu Shay' is Arabic, and in English in means "all things". Man is a witness to the creation of all things, himself included. No one can doubt that the 19th and 20th centuries are indeed a black and ruinous age. The great world wars and atomic and hydrogen weapons will cause future generations of men to call these generations the most barbaric people that have ever lived upon the earth. In the past we would condemn the primitive peoples for sacrificing a young man or woman to the God of fertility and yet this 20th century has seen mankind take hundreds of thousands of people and sacrifice them to the God of war.

The Excellent Temple is the Manifestation of God, Bahá'u'lláh, and He indeed has a wondrous voice for it is the very voice of God speaking through His Teacher. The

Apex refers to the very highest place or station. So not only does God speak to, and teach us, but He does so from the highest point of eternity.

The end result and purpose of God speaking to us through the Manifestation seems to be indicated here, that is, so man can by his own independent efforts attain to a godly and spiritual station and life. This spiritual fruition in man can be made possible by his acknowledgment of the oneness and glory of his Creator. Once man acknowledges the Teacher, then that man must follow the Teachings to the letter.

When one looks upon creation, all things reflect the handiwork of our Creator. The sky, sun, clouds, the waterfall, the rainbow, man, animals, flowers and all plant and sea life and all of nature are evidences of a love for beauty and creation and are proof of our Creator.

> *And I praise and glorify the first sea which hath branched from the ocean of the Divine Essence, and the first morn which hath glowed from the Horizon of Oneness, and the first sun which hath risen in the Heaven of Eternity, and the first fire which was lit from the Lamp of Preexistence in the lantern of singleness: He who was Ahmad in the kingdom of the exalted ones, and Muhammad amongst the concourse of the near ones, and Mahmúd in the realm of the sincere ones. "... by whichsoever (name) ye will, invoke Him: He hath most excellent names" in the hearts of those who know. And upon His household and companions be abundant and abiding and eternal peace!*

In this passage it seems that Bahá'u'lláh is giving praise to the acts of primal creation. We know from the writings of Bahá'u'lláh that creation has always existed and will always exist. So the first sea, the first morn, the first sun, the first fire that came forth from God could be referring to the Manifestation and is a spiritual truth. It is through these wonderful Teachers that the ocean of understanding surges in the human heart. The morning light of divine guidance lights up the heart of man, and so forth.

This could also signify the birth of a baby from the womb of its mother, for each person it is the first morn, the first sea etc.

He praises Muhammad in a glowing tribute. The name Ahmad, Muhammad, and Mahmúd are names used for Muhammad and signify praise and exaltation. He also points out that whatever name one uses for God is the most excellent name. He also gives to the true followers of Muhammad a promise of eternal peace.

> *Further, we have harkened to what the nightingale of knowledge sang on the boughs of the tree of thy being, and learned what the dove of certitude cried on the branches of the bower of thy heart. Methinks I verily inhaled the pure fragrances of the garment of thy love, and attained thy very meeting from perusing thy letter. And since I noted thy mention of thy death in God, and thy life through Him, and thy love for the beloved of God and the Manifestations of His Names and the Dawning-Points of His Attributes—I therefore reveal unto thee sacred and resplendent tokens from the planes of glory, to attract thee into the court of holiness and nearness and beauty, and draw thee to a station wherein thou shalt see nothing in creation save the Face of thy Beloved One, the Honored, and behold all created things only as in the day wherein none hath a mention.*

This is an example of the great poetic and exalted way in which Bahá'u'lláh wrote. Here He tells the Sufi mystic that through this Book he will draw near unto God and become a holy and spiritual being. It also tells us where this Book is coming from.

From the letter that the Sufi wrote to Bahá'u'lláh He was able to determine the Sufi's deep feelings and his sincerity towards God and Bahá'u'lláh. He then seems to explain that what He is going to reveal to the Sufi in the

Seven Valleys will attract him to a spiritual station of absolute certitude. The person that goes through the Seven Valleys will reach a station where nothing will be, or could be mentioned except God.

Bahá'u'lláh often refers to Himself as a nightingale. As all knowledge comes from the knowledge of God so this is the song of God that touches the heart of man. Also a nightingale sings in the beauty of the rose garden at night, so it is with the Great Teachers from God. They also come to us in the darkness of the night of ignorance and disbelief. They always come after the light of the previous teacher has almost gone out. In this day as stated above "this black and ruinous age".

The Sufi Bahá'u'lláh is addressing was no doubt certain in his belief and sincere. The dove from the time of Noah was a bird of safety, security and peace. As the story from the Old Testament says in Genesis:

> "Also he sent forth a dove from him, to see if the waters were abated from off the face of the ground;
>
> But the dove found no rest for the sole of her foot, and she returned unto him into the ark, for the waters were on the face of the whole earth.
>
> And he stayed yet other seven days; and again he sent forth the dove out of the ark;
>
> And the dove came in to him in the evening; and, lo, in her mouth was an olive leaf plucked off: so Noah knew that the waters were abated from off the earth."

This dove referred to by Bahá'u'lláh is no ordinary dove but a dove of certitude that is settled in the center of one's heart. The word certitude means that you are absolutely certain of the truth of Bahá'u'lláh.

By reading the Sufi's letter Bahá'u'lláh was able to sense this man's love and sincerity. He often uses fragrance because a fragrance can be diffused in all directions. For example, if I open a bottle of very fragrant perfume the odor soon permeates the whole house. So it is with the words of God, once released by the Messenger they soon permeate all mankind. This no doubt refers to the sacrifice of one's self to the point of the self's nonexistence and the reality of true life which can only be attained through absolute obedience to the will of God. There is also an indication of the fact that to truly love God is to truly love one's fellow man. To love God is also to love His Manifestation. Bahá'u'lláh is the Manifestation of His Names and the Dawning-Points of His Attributes in this day.

What Bahá'u'lláh reveals to us and the tokens mentioned is this present work "The Seven valley". The purpose of this Book is the development of man's true spiritual nature. He also tells us where these tokens or this Book came from, which is the plane of glory or heaven sent.

> Of this hath the nightingale of oneness sung in the garden of Ghawthíyyih. He saith: "And there shall appear upon the Tablet of thine heart a writing of the subtle mysteries of 'Fear God and God will give you knowledge'; and the bird of thy soul shall recall the holy sanctuaries of preexistence and soar on the wings of longing in the heaven of 'walk the beaten paths of thy Lord', and gather the fruits of communion in the gardens of 'Then feed on every kind of fruit'."

Ghawthíyyih refers to unseen angels, it was also a garden where Alí the son-in-law of Muhammad talked to his followers. Evidently Bahá'u'lláh is referring to what Alí said in that garden. As the heart is the organ of feeling and sensitivity, anything written on the Tablet of ones heart would be felt and sensed rather than understood with the mind. If one truly fears displeasing God then that one will be on the road to true knowledge. Of course all of this is very mysterious to us mortals.

It is clearly written that we all have come from God and we will surely return to Him.

> "All men have proceeded from God and unto Him shall all return." (The Báb: Selections from the Báb, page 157)

To soar on the wings of longing is a spiritual condition. Although a man is walking, living and breathing on this earth his soul is far and away soaring in the revelation of his Creator.

Walk the beaten paths of thy Lord seems to mean follow the road signs on this highway of life, which is the instructions that have come from God. When the road sign says stop we had better stop, when the sign says go we had better go and when the sign says caution we sure had better be careful.

To gather the fruits of communion is an interesting statement because communion is a deeply felt prayer and prayer and meditation are required for true communion to take place. Prayer is our side of this communion, or us speaking, and meditation is His side of the communion where we must listen with heart and soul to what He is saying. When we do this we are nourishing our souls with the heavenly fruit.

Bahá'u'lláh further states where this Book is taking us. We can just get a glimmer of such an exalted station.

> By My life, O friend, wert thou to taste of these fruits, from the green garden of these blossoms which grow in the lands of knowledge, beside the orient lights of the Essence in the mirrors of names and attributes—yearning would seize the reins of patience and reserve from out thy hand, and make thy soul to shake with the flashing light, and draw thee from the earthly homeland to the first, heavenly abode in the Center of Realities, and lift thee to a plane wherein thou wouldst soar in the air even as thou walkest upon the earth, and move over the water as thou runnest on the land. Wherefore, may it rejoice Me, and thee, and whosoever mounteth into the heaven of knowledge, and whose heart is refreshed by this, that the wind of

> certitude hath blown over the garden of his being, from the Sheba of the All-Merciful.
>
> Peace be upon him who followeth the Right Path!

To taste of the fruits is to assimilate them into our lives and the green garden of these blossoms seem to indicate a living and growing garden. So the Teachings of God should be a living and growing part of our lives.

The orient lights could mean that the lights of the knowledge of God, like the rising sun, comes up in the east. The unknowable Essence is mirrored to mankind from the Manifestation of the names and attributes of the Essence Itself.

If man could just get a small taste of the reality of the knowledge of God, the yearning of man's soul to have more would overwhelm him.

Light and enlightenment usually refer to knowledge. The soul is man's reality, and should it penetrate into the knowledge of his Creator it would be like an earthquake shaking his inmost being. When this light begins to dawn it will pull man away from this world and its empty and vain pursuits and set him on the road to his true and heavenly home which exists in the Center of Realities. The Center of Realities is Bahá'u'lláh.

Air is a life giving element to all that live on earth and the Words of God are the life giving elements of man's spiritual life. So to soar in the air could mean to soar into the teachings. To move over the water is to move over the sea of life and not get our feet wet in the earthly waters of vain and selfish desires.

Bahá'u'lláh here tells us that it will make Him happy and it will make us happy also as we ascend into the knowledge of God. Our hearts will become refreshed through this knowledge. Our inner and outer beings will become absolutely assured and certain of the truth of this revelation.

Sheba is an interesting word. The Queen of Sheba, so the story goes, was the Queen of Ethiopia who came to visit King Solomon, the wise. Although she was a sun worshiper she became a firm believer in the oneness of God. It was believed that she came from a land of great wealth and beauty in the physical sense, Bahá'u'lláh uses this phrase quite often and it seems to mean from the spiritual land of great spiritual wealth and spiritual beauty.

This statement is a closing salutation to the letter and indicates that the main theme "The Seven Valleys" is the right path to follow.

We have to understand that the Manifestation of God, Bahá'u'lláh, uses physical terms that we understand to convey a very spiritual meaning. If we were to taste of these fruits which are His Teachings and get even a little understanding of them, our souls would soar into heaven even as our physical bodies walk upon the earth.

And further: The stages that mark the wayfarer's journey from the abode of dust to the heavenly homeland are said to be seven. Some have called these Seven Valleys, and others, Seven Cities. And they say that until the wayfarer taketh leave of self and traverseth these stages, he shall never reach to the ocean of nearness and union, nor drink of the peerless wine. The first is—

THE VALLEY OF SEARCH

The steed of this Valley is patience; without patience the wayfarer on this journey will reach nowhere and attain no goal. Nor should he ever be downhearted; if he strive for a hundred thousand years and yet fail to behold the beauty of the Friend, he should not falter. For those who seek the Ka'bih of "for Us" rejoice in the tidings: "In Our ways will We guide them". In their search, they have stoutly girded up the loins of service, and seek at every moment to journey from the plane of heedlessness into the realm of being. No bond shall hold them back, and no counsel shall deter them.

This seems to indicate that we must pass through seven stages of life. The maturing of the human soul will require these seven steps or seven stages of its development.

A wayfarer is a person who is on the way to a destination or goal but does not know where it is or how to get there. The journey's goal is from the world of materialism, or dust, to heaven which is man's true home.

If we think about a valley we must go down into the valley and then climb up the other side. Also seven cities means enter and leave the city. In a valley or city it is easy to become distracted, by the beauty of the valley or the materialism of the city.

The traveler must get rid of his excess baggage, that is his own self if he wishes to make the trip. Unless we are willing to give up our ideas, our acquired knowledge, our greed and self centeredness we can never get near to God or drink the peerless wine of understanding, His teachings. Peerless means the best with no equal. Peerless wine is unequalled wine in which man becomes intoxicated with the love of God.

In order to go through this valley of search we need a horse, and a steed is not an ordinary horse. A steed is a horse of great strength and speed. Yet this fast horse is named patience. I pray every day for patience. "O God! give me patience, right now!"

Unless we can acquire this attribute of patience we can never hope to reach Bahá'u'lláh and we will never reach our goal in life.

If we were to live for a hundred thousand years and still not reach our goal of nearness to God, we must not be discouraged or become downhearted.

To falter means to misstep. It also could mean to hesitate and not to be certain of what we are doing.

Ka'bih is a place in Mecca (Arabic, "a square building"), Islám's most sacred sanctuary and pilgrimage shrine, it is located in the courtyard of the Great Mosque of Mecca. A trough in which they reputedly mixed mortar stands near the door and is a popular place of prayer. The

Ka'bih houses the Black Stone, the most venerated object for Muslims. After the Prophet established control of Mecca, the shrine was rededicated to Alláh. All Muslims face toward the Ka'bih during their daily prayers. All Muslim men must in their lifetime visit the Ka'bih. So it is truly the goal of life.

This implies that the goal when attained will be worth whatever effort we put into the search. We also have a wonderful assurance here, Bahá'u'lláh says that if we only make the effort God will guide us and if God guides us we will surely attain our goal. This word Ka'bih means goal.

When one enters this valley of search it means that the seeker must also be of service to the world of man for he must gird up the loins of service. Not just service but strong service. The loins of man are that part of his body above the hips and below the rib cage on his side. In the days of doing battle with swords, the first part to weaken was a man's loins. A soldier would then put on a strong wide, leather girdle to support his loins. This is where we get the term to "gird up your loins".

The plane of heedlessness is non-existence because the opposite is the kingdom of existence. The bonds are ropes or ties that bind us. For example, the bond of friends, relatives and work are all barriers for our spiritual progress. Our friends and relations will counsel us to not go, or not seek and try to dissuade us from our journey.

Bahá'u'lláh says here that we must be firm in our resolve to seek and find God.

> *It is incumbent on these servants that they cleanse the heart—which is the wellspring of divine treasures—from every marking, and that they turn away from imitation, which is following the traces of their forefathers and sires, and shut the door of friendliness and enmity upon all the people of the earth.*

Incumbent means that we must do it, that is we must clean up our hearts.

A wellspring is a spring of fresh clean water that bubbles up out of the ground and the more one uses the water, more water flows from the spring. Another thing about a wellspring is that if you don't use the water it will clog up and eventually stop flowing entirely. So here we must clean and purify our hearts so that the divine treasures that God has created within us can flow out. Some of the debris that will clog up our hearts are markings of imagination, imitating other people and following in the footsteps of our ancestors without checking it out for the truth. Bahá'u'lláh points out here that both friends and enemies can hold us back from our journey. For example, a person is seriously searching for God, but this person is also very prejudiced about black people. One day, he meets a black person that has the knowledge of the road he must take to reach his goal but because the man is black he doesn't listen and misses the chance.

> In this journey the seeker reacheth a stage wherein he seeth all created things wandering distracted in search of the Friend. How many a Jacob will he see, hunting after his Joseph; he will behold many a lover, hastening to seek the Beloved, he will witness a world of desiring ones searching after the One Desired. At every moment he findeth a weighty matter, in every hour he becometh aware of a mystery; for he hath taken his heart away from both worlds, and set out for the Ka'bih of the Beloved. At every step, aid from the Invisible Realm will attend him and the heat of his search will grow.

This is an interesting statement that all created things are in search of God. He also states that they are wandering distracted in search of the Friend. They are distracted by job, money, drugs, sex, TV, vacations and all material pursuits.

This story of Jacob and Joseph has been related in the Bible and also in the Qur'án. Bahá'u'lláh refers to this in many of His writings. The following story is taken from the Old Testament and the Qur'án.

Once upon a time, ever so long ago, there lived in the land of Canaan a man called Jacob. Jacob had worked for Leban, his father-in-law, for seven long years in hopes of having Leban's daughter, the beautiful Ráchel for a bride. Jacob truly loved Rachel. He served his father-in-law faithfully. He was out in the fields in the cold of winter and the heat of summer and many the night he went without sleep tending the flocks of his father-in-law. However, on the wedding night he was cheated by Leban and was forced to marry Rachel's elder sister Leah. Jacob still had a great love for Rachel. He agreed to work for Leban another seven years for her. Then through more cheating, Leban got another six years of service out of Jacob. In total Jacob served Leban for 20 years. God, however was aware of the subterfuge and cheating of Leban and so when Leban said Jacob could have all the spotted lambs and kids from the flocks, all the sheep and goats had spotted lambs and kids. Leban then changed his mind and said that Jacob could have all the streaked ones, all the flocks produced streaked animals. Leban then said Jacob could have all the dark animals, then only dark ones were born. As a result Jacob left his father-in-law a very wealthy man.

After fourteen years of marriage, Rachel had a son. She named the baby Joseph and six years later Rachel gave birth a second time and died in childbirth. This baby was named Benjamin and was Joseph's younger brother. The other ten sons of Jacob were only Joseph's half brothers.

As a baby Joseph seldom cried and was indeed a most beautiful child. He loved his brothers deeply and always shared with them whatever he had. Joseph above all loved his father and he was very religious by nature. His religion was not just a bigoted following of rituals and forms but was in itself a love of life and living. When God said be gentle, loving, kind, generous and faithful little Joseph tried. As a result, Jacob loved Joseph more than all the other children, his greatest joy was to be with him. Joseph was indeed a prince and he lived the life of a prince. The finest food, clothing and luxuries were bestowed upon him. While the other brothers worked in the fields and tended the flocks of Jacob, only Joseph was exempt. Of course, Benjamin was too little to do anything. When Joseph was in his teens, he delighted in the countryside. He had a deep love and respect for nature and the Creator of nature. The jealousy of his brothers knew no bounds, to add to their envy and hate, Joseph began to have dreams.

His first disturbing dream was one where all of his brothers were in the field binding sheaves of wheat, all of a sudden Joseph's sheaf stood up and all his brothers sheaves gathered around and bowed down to Joseph's sheaf. This of course further inflamed the hatred of Joseph's brothers.

The next dream was about eleven stars and the moon and the sun even, all bowing down to Joseph. The ten elder brothers vowed that they would get even with this egotistical brother who thought that he was so great that even Joseph's father and mother would bow down to him. Jacob, was convinced that his precious son would one day be ruler of them all.

Now everyday the ten brothers schemed and plotted as to how they could get Joseph. They went to Jacob and complained that Joseph was now almost 17 years old and knew nothing about the livestock or the planting and harvesting of the fields. Jacob had misgivings about allowing Joseph to go and so he steadfastly refused. The brothers conceived a plan to get all the servants out of the house and into the fields and then when they went to tend the flocks they would forget to take their supplies. They knew that Jacob would then send the apple of his eye, Joseph, to them with the supplies. Their nefarious scheme worked. Jacob put on Joseph a new coat made of many colours and sent him off to his brothers with the supplies.

The brothers recognized the coming of Joseph far off because of the coat of many colours and were delighted. "Now we can kill that dreamer and our father will love us as he has loved Joseph," they said. They were unaware of that most basic of truths, love can't be forced but is freely given and earned by the behaviour of the beloved one.

A fierce quarrel ensued among the ten brothers. All wanted Joseph killed, but none wanted his blood on their hands. Finally, it was agreed that they would, for the time being, put him in an abandoned cistern nearby. This pit was once used as an underground storage tank for water and was now dry. So they fell upon Joseph and threw him into this underground pit. They took his coat of many colours and rent and tore it then dipped it into the blood of a freshly killed lamb.

This quarrel of the brothers continued for many days, while poor Joseph languished in the pit. Then one day, as they were quarreling, in the distance they saw a caravan of merchants coming. They were traveling to some far-off land. It was as if providence had given the brothers a solution, as indeed it had. The brothers agreed, "We can sell Joseph as a slave to these merchants, make a few bucks and be rid of Joseph in the bargain." This solution pleased them all. Joseph was pulled out of the cistern, chained and sold to the caravan as a slave for 30 pieces of silver. Each brother received three pieces of silver and in this way the guilt was shared by them all.

The brothers took the bloody and torn coat of Joseph home to their father and told him, that Joseph must have been killed by wild animals in the wilderness. Jacob did not for one minute believe his sons and he cried out in pain and anguish, "What have you done to my Joseph, where is he?"

From that time on, Jacob could not be comforted, and when ever he thought of Joseph he wept. In fact he wept so much for his lost Joseph over the years that in the end he became blind.

The caravan that had bought Joseph slowly made its way from place to place, and finally arrived in far off Egypt. Joseph slowly won over all of his captors with his gentle manner and loving heart. The merchants agreed to find Joseph a good master and a good home in Egypt. Joseph in his heart felt that he was sent to Egypt by God and for God's purpose, so he was not unhappy nor was he bitter towards his brothers. Joseph was sold to the Pharaoh's captain of the guard. He was a good and honest man and the merchants knew Joseph would be well-treated by this good man.

Joseph went to work with a will and was sure that God was indeed with him. What God said do, Joseph did, and what God said not to do, Joseph refused to do. He always kept his word and fulfilled his promises and obligations, he was gentle and kind to the extreme not only with his owner, the Captain, but also with his household and the other slaves. Everyone grew to love him and to trust him. As a result, the Captain gave Joseph more and more responsibility until at last he was put in charge of all of the Captain's affairs. He ran the house, the fields and took care of all the business for his owner. Because he worked hard in the fields with the other slaves, his body filled out. He became strong in body as he already was in spirit. As he had been a beautiful baby, child and youth, he now became a truly beautiful man. You could say he was the most handsome man in Egypt and the word would not do justice to Joseph.

The wife of the Captain fell madly in love with Joseph and she used every womanly wile she could to seduce him. However, Joseph being true to himself and as ever true to God was incorruptible. As this woman had a very high social position, she had many friends and soon her friends discovered her secret infatuation with Joseph and teased her about falling in love with a Hebrew slave. So the Captain's wife put on a big luncheon and invited all these friends to come. After lunch, tea was served with oranges and each of the guests was given a knife in order to peal their oranges.

She also arranged for Joseph to come in at this time. All the ladies at the table cut their hands because they were so overcome by the beauty of Joseph. The Captain's wife then chided her friends and they agreed that it would be impossible to not fall in love with such a wonderful man.

This woman was determined that she would have her way with Joseph. She sent all the servants from the house at a time when she knew Joseph would be coming to take care of the household affairs. She took off her clothes and when Joseph came in she called to him from the bed room to come. Unsuspecting, Joseph always the obedient servant, went into the bed room. She grabbed hold of his coat and insisted that he make love to her. Joseph told her that this he could never do, didn't his master trust him with all of his affairs, didn't he give Joseph complete control over everything he owned. His wife, Joseph could never violate and adultery was against the laws of God. This woman overcome by her desire struggled with Joseph. She grabbed onto his coat. He slipped out of his coat and left the house. The Captain's wife felt rejected and scorned and was humiliated by this refusal of a slave to obey her. She tore her clothes and screamed, "Rape! rape!"

When the servants came running, they saw Joseph running from the house, the woman clutching his coat, naked with torn clothes. It was an open and shut case against Joseph. The Captain threw Joseph into the prison of the Pharaoh.

Soon Joseph was forgotten in the prison where he was forced to stay. Joseph still felt that he was under the protection of God and was in this prison to do God's will. He was by nature a happy being. As the years went by, Joseph spent his time in prayer, meditation and study. He also spent much time in caring for the other prisoners, trying to make their hard lives a little easier.

The chief cupbearer and the chief baker, who had offended the Pharaoh, were also in the prison. One day they came to Joseph and asked him to explain their dreams. The cupbearer said, "Last night in my dream I saw a grape vine with three branches and as I watched it budded, blossomed and the grapes ripened. As I was holding the Pharaoh's cup in my hand, I took the bunches of grapes and squeezed them into Pharaoh's cup and put the full cup into Pharaoh's hand."

Joseph explained, "The three branches were three days, so in three days you will be taken from the prison and restored to your position as chief cupbearer to the Pharaoh. Please remember me to the Pharaoh as I am an innocent man, stolen from my home, sold into slavery and now unjustly imprisoned."

The cupbearer promised Joseph that if his explanation of the dream was correct, he would surely tell his Pharaoh about him.

The chief baker then told Joseph his dream. He said, "Last night in my dream, I was carrying on my head three baskets of bread. The top basket was filled with all kinds of bakery goods, but the birds were eating them."

Joseph explained, "The three baskets are three days. In three days you will be taken out of the prison and your head will be cut off and hung on the palace gate where the birds will feed on it."

So it all happened just as Joseph said it would, but the cupbearer forgot his promise to Joseph and he remained in the prison for another two years.

Pharaoh started to have a recurring dream and he began to fret and worry about it, until it became an obsession. All his soothsayers, magicians and priests could not give the Pharaoh a satisfactory explanation. At long last the negligent cupbearer remembered Joseph and his promise to him. He told the Pharaoh about Joseph down in the dungeon and Joseph's story. So Joseph was hauled out of the prison, bathed, perfumed and given new clothes and taken to the Pharaoh. The wife of the Captain of the guard was called in. This woman had suffered a great deal with her conscience. Joseph had always been not only a faithful servant of her family, but also an upright and honest man. So when the Pharaoh questioned her she told the truth and through her tears vindicated Joseph. The Pharaoh left her punishment to Joseph and he instantly forgave her and told her that she was just doing God's will. The Pharaoh then sent her back to her family and the wrath of her husband.

The Pharaoh then told Joseph his dreams, "I was standing in the field and there were seven sheaves of wheat. Their stalks were full and golden. Then I saw seven other sheaves of grain. They came up out of the ground, but they were sick and gaunt. They had little or no kernels of grain on them and they ate up the seven healthy and full sheaves, but remained as sick as ever."

"In my other dream", he said, "I was again in the field and there were seven fat, sleek and healthy cows. Then I saw seven sick, gaunt, starved and ugly cows come up out of the ground and devour the good animals, but they remained as thin and ugly as before."

Joseph told the Pharaoh that these dreams were one and the same. God was sending the Pharaoh a warning. There would be seven years of plenty, the harvests would be the best ever. These years would be followed by seven years of famine. Death and starvation would stalk the land and for the seven years there would be no relief.

Pharaoh asked Joseph what could be done. Joseph told Pharaoh that during the years of plenty, they must, through a tax program, collect the produce of the land and save it to be used during the years of famine. Warehouses and granaries had to be built and no time could be lost. The Captain of the guard then told Pharaoh that Joseph was the best man to oversee this program. He further explained that under the management of Joseph his affairs had never been handled so well. The heads of state agreed with the Captain and so the Pharaoh made Joseph his Prime Minister. He put his signet ring on the hand of Joseph. No one, except Pharaoh, had more authority. Joseph was given a palace and he took a wife and as was his custom, he went to work with a will.

Never in the history of man had there been such harvests. Joseph took a tax of 20% and the Pharaoh's warehouses and granaries were full to overflowing. The builders were hard pressed to keep up with the abundant harvests. The first seven years went by quickly. Then as Joseph had said, the seven years of famine started with a vengeance. The famine extended over the whole area even into Israel. The only place food could be purchased was in Egypt.

Back in Israel, Jacob finally had to send his sons to Egypt to purchase food. He only kept Benjamin at home with him. The ten sons took their animals and made up a caravan and went off to Egypt. When they arrived in Egypt, Joseph recognized his brothers at once, but they did not recognize Joseph. Joseph was seventeen years old when he was sold into slavery, he was in his early twenties when he was thrown into the prison and was thirty years old when he became the Prime Minister of Egypt. Joseph was about 38 years old when his brothers came to Egypt. The brothers all bowed themselves to the ground, in respect to the supreme lord of Egypt. Joseph questioned his brothers and learned that his father had gone blind weeping for his lost son. Joseph was so overcome with love for his family that he excused himself and went into his private chambers and wept.

He treated his brothers very harshly and they became terrified of him. He then instructed his agents to load up the caravan to its capacity and to put the silver they had brought for payment back into the sacks of grain. He then called his brothers to him and told them that if they returned again to Egypt, they must bring their younger brother Benjamin with them. If they came without him, they would be considered spies and put into the dungeon. Joseph then sent them on their way.

After they returned home, they discovered all their silver in their sacks. They were elated, and when they told their father about this prince of Egypt and his demands that they bring Benjamin with them on their next visit. Jacob declared that in that event there would be no other trips to Egypt.

The famine unrelentingly continued and all the supplies were soon exhausted. Jacob's sons pleaded with their father to let them return to Egypt. Even if it meant going to prison for stealing the Pharaoh's silver. Jacob refused and death and starvation stalked the land. Finally the brothers argued with their father that even his beloved Benjamin would be dead. They would be unable to make another trip because all the animals would also be gone. Jacob relented only when his sons guaranteed the safety of Benjamin, with their own lives. They took an oath to that effect.

Once more in Egypt, Joseph put on a big banquet for his brothers at his palace. When their caravan was being loaded, Joseph instructed his steward to put his silver cup from his table in the sack of Benjamin. When the brothers came into the presence of the Lord of Egypt they prostrated themselves to the ground and implored Joseph to have mercy upon them as they did not intend to steal his money and they now brought double in order to make full payment. Joseph told them to keep their money. They had now shown good faith by bringing their youngest brother to him, so he would not charge them anything. They then enjoyed the banquet and the hospitality of Joseph.

The next morning the caravan left for home. It had only gone a few miles when Pharaoh's soldiers overtook them and forced them to return. Joseph explained that his silver cup was missing and it was unthinkable that these Hebrews would repay his kindness by stealing it even after he had freely given them a banquet and their supplies. The brothers one and all declared their innocence. Joseph told them that if this cup was found in their possession the thief would become his slave. The brothers unanimously agreed and the search of their property soon yielded the silver cup in Benjamin's possession. The bothers told Joseph that they would all stay as slaves, but he must let Benjamin go as if he did not return it would surely kill their old father.

Joseph refused but he took off his shirt and gave it to the brothers and said, "Give this to your father when you tell him about Benjamin and he will not die". He then sent them on their way.

The borther's joy was now turned into sorrow and they wept all the way home. They were sure that this was God's punishment for having done away with Joseph so many years ago. Now they must kill their father by having betrayed their oaths about the loss of Benjamin also. They were sure he would die of grief over this loss.

When his sons told him what happened in Egypt and gave him the shirt of the prince of Egypt, he held it up to his nose inhaled deeply and cried out, "My Joseph lives! my Joseph lives!" He recognized his long lost Joseph from the fragrance of his shirt. Jacob then took his family and went to his son in Egypt.

The Egypt of love, the land of reunion with the Beloved and the land of plenty. This story is a wonderful allegorical story of life, living and the search for God. Joseph is that light of God or Spirit of God that from time to time comes into the earth to shed God's light upon man and teach him about his true self. The brothers represent the generality of mankind. We reject our Lord from selfish desires and for material gain. Joseph ever loving, ever forgiving and the Beloved One, even when crucified, imprisoned, mocked and humiliated, still loves His brothers and yearns for their eternal happiness.

As the seeker or wayfarer moves along in the Valley of Search, he will find others like himself seeking the Beloved (Bahá'u'lláh) and the One Desired. This should give heart to the Bahá'í teacher when he thinks that no one is interested and no one can be found to teach.

Can anyone imagine a more weighty matter or a mystery greater than the matter and mystery of the purpose of life and the Creator of life? Yet if we are truly in the Valley of Search it seems that these things are revealed to us.

The idea is to take ones heart away from both worlds in order to seek our goal. It is claimed that this Ka'bih was the first temple built by Adam and reconstructed after the flood by Abraham. In this building is the Black Stone, which, it is said was delivered by the angel Gabriel to Abraham and Ishmael from Paradise. It is the goal of every Muslim man to visit this shrine during his lifetime. Bahá'u'lláh uses this term, Ka'bih to refer to Himself and He indeed is the Goal of all Goals.

This seems to indicate that one's motive to find God must not be for one's own gain neither for material gain nor for spiritual gain. One thing about The Seven Valleys of Bahá'u'lláh is that He is constantly assuring and reassuring us. This passage tells us that as long as we are taking steps, aid from the invisible Realm will be given and the fire started in our hearts will increase. Stepping indicates that we are in motion.

> *One must judge of search by the standard of the Majnún of Love. It is related that one day they came upon Majnún sifting the dust, and his tears flowing down. They said, "What doest thou?" He said, "I seek for Laylí". They cried, "Alas for thee! Laylí is of pure spirit, and thou seekest her in the dust!" He said, "I seek her everywhere; haply somewhere I shall find her."*
>
> *Yea, although to the wise it be shameful to seek the Lord of Lords in the dust, yet this betokeneth intense ardor in searching. "Whoso seeketh out a thing with zeal shall find it."*

Majnún means an insane man and mankind is like this Majnún. We still use the terms all the time, like a person is madly in love or I am crazy about someone.

Mankind looks for spiritual truth in magic, drugs, sex, alcohol and even suicide. Truly they are looking in the dust but even when we do this and our search for God is sincere, God again assures us that we shall find Him. Laylí in this story seems to mean the spirit of man and as a gift from God, the spirit should be pure.

Bahá'u'lláh says that, yes, a wise man would not be looking for God in the dust and for a wise man to do this would be a shameful act. He further explains that if we put our hearts into the search and are zealous in our search even if we are looking in the wrong places we will find what we are looking for.

> The true seeker hunteth naught but the object of his quest, and the lover hath no desire save union with his beloved. Nor shall the seeker reach his goal unless he sacrifice all things. That is, whatever he hath seen, and heard, and understood, all must he set at naught, that he may enter the realm of the spirit, which is the City of God. Labor is needed, if we are to seek Him; ardor is needed, if we are to drink of the honey of reunion with Him; and if we taste of this cup, we shall cast away the world.

To be a true seeker we must be single-minded in our quest. To be a true lover we must have no desire except a desire to be united with God.

Here we are informed that in order to reach our goal we must sacrifice all the manmade things that we have acquired. Not only the material things one has but also everything one has seen, heard and understood. If and when we can do this and clear ourselves of all our preconceived ideas then we will be in the realm of the spirit and worthy to enter the City of God.

He also tells us that labor and ardor are needed. Labor is not just work but indicates hard work and ardor means we must put our heart into it. Then when a soul gets just a tiny taste of the nearness of God, that soul will never be satisfied with anything else. We would throw away the world with all its riches.

> On this journey the traveler abideth in every land and dwelleth in every region. In every face, he seeketh the beauty of the Friend; in every country he looketh for the Beloved. He joineth every company, and seeketh fellowship with every soul, that haply in some mind he may uncover the secret of the Friend, or in some face he may behold the beauty of the Loved One.

The seeker must be willing to look everywhere and investigate every lead if he is to reach the goal. It also indicates that we must be in motion and willing to go wherever we need to in our quest. It also indicates that we must not be rushing here and there but should be willing to abide long enough to be able to find our Beloved.

Bahá'u'lláh tells us that His Beauty is hidden beyond a myriad veils. So unless a person is willing to set aside ones prejudices and seek with an open mind and an open heart he will never find his goal.

> *And if, by the help of God, he findeth on this journey a trace of the traceless Friend, and inhaleth the fragrance of the long-lost Joseph from the heavenly messenger, he shall straightway step into*

THE VALLEY OF LOVE

> *and be dissolved in the fire of love. In this city the heaven of ecstasy is upraised and the world-illumining sun of yearning shineth, and the fire of love is ablaze; and when the fire of love is ablaze, it burneth to ashes the harvest of reason.*

You will remember from the story of Joseph that although Jacob had gone blind he recognized his beloved Joseph from the fragrance of his shirt. The traceless Friend is God and no trace of Him can be found except in His Messenger who will and does help us. If God does not help us our journey is doomed to failure.

When sugar is dissolved in water, the water still looks like water but it has taken on the sweetness of the sugar. The sugar must give up its granular qualities and take on the qualities of the water. When we enter into the valley of the fire of love we must give up ourselves and become one with the fire. Another good example is iron. It is cold and hard but when put into the fire it becomes soft and fluid and takes on all the qualities of the fire. This fire is the fire of the love of God, which is the most intense fire.

The lover yearns to be with the one loved. Love is a feeling, an emotion that can't be explained, it can only be felt, because it deals only with the heart. A person in love becomes ecstatic. Ecstasy is the very highest form of happiness and joy.

Bahá'u'lláh here states that in the fire of love the harvest of reason is burned to ashes. Reason is not burned only the harvest of reason is burned. A harvest is all the past reasoning. It's like one has a field of rice and mixed into the rice are weeds, in fact, so many weeds that the farmer just burns the field so that he can replant and then harvest a good field. True and pure love must consume all the man-made reasons and vain imaginations man has acquired.

> Now is the traveler unaware of himself, and of aught besides himself. He seeth neither ignorance nor knowledge, neither doubt nor certitude; he knoweth not the morn of guidance from the night of error. He fleeth both from unbelief and faith, and deadly poison is a balm to him. Wherefore Áttár saith:
>
> For the infidel, error—for the faithful, faith;
> For Áttár's heart, an atom of Thy pain.

A person in love can't think of anyone or anything except the one that is loved. In this state the lover does not think of himself but in reality is thinking only of himself by being in the presence of the one he loves. Because of this all consuming love his mind is confused and knowledge and ignorance are indistinguishable. In this state he also runs away from faith and no faith. Even if he was to take poison he would consider it a healing medicine because in the state of an all consuming love the reality is completely confused.

> The steed of this Valley is pain; and if there be no pain this journey will never end. In this station the lover hath no thought save the Beloved, and seeketh no refuge save the Friend. At every moment he

> offereth a hundred lives in the path of the Loved One, at every step he throweth a thousand heads at the feet of the Beloved.

The transport to get us through this valley is pain. Now all we have is just a trace of God and this sets our hearts afire with love for Him. The greatest pain is being separated from the one you love, but like Áttár one would not exchange this love for anything and the pain of separation increases our love. If I had a hundred lives and a thousand heads I would willingly give them all to my beloved.

> O My Brother! Until thou enter the Egypt of love, thou shalt never come to the Joseph of the Beauty of the Friend; and until, like Jacob, thou forsake thine outward eyes, thou shalt never open the eye of thine inward being; and until thou burn with the fire of love, thou shalt never commune with the Lover of Longing.

This inner eye is the eye of the spirit. To commune is a communication at a very deep level and the one we will commune with is the Lover of Longing which is God.

> A lover feareth nothing and no harm can come nigh him:
> Thou seest him chill in the fire and dry in the sea.
> A lover is he who is chill in hell fire;
> A knower is he who is dry in the sea.

This love is a protection and even if thrown into fire or into the sea, he would be protected, surrounded by the love of God. This is a wonderful assurance from Bahá'u'lláh that if one is a true lover of God, that one would fear nothing and no person or thing could harm him.

> Love accepteth no existence and wisheth no life; He seeth life in death, and in shame seeketh glory. To merit the madness of love, man must abound in sanity; to merit the bonds of the Friend, he must be

> *full of spirit. Blessed the neck that is caught in His noose, happy the head that falleth on the dust in the pathway of His love. Wherefore, O friend, give up thy self that thou mayest find the Peerless One, pass by this mortal earth that thou mayest seek a home in the nest of heaven. Be as naught, if thou wouldst kindle the fire of being and be fit for the pathway of love.*

The true lovers of God are considered to be mad, yet when we look at this we see that they are the only sane people on earth, where most people are seeking for pleasure, lying, cheating, stealing and are selfish and greedy and working for their own special interests. The ones who really try to follow the Teachings of God are loving, kind, gentle, truthful, sharing and working for unity and peace. Often when a person falls deeply into love we say that they are madly in love. In this state they seem to have lost their minds. Now would you rather be a beautiful person with a beautiful soul and possess a pure, kindly and radiant heart, or a person greedy, selfish and possess a black, corrupt and polluted heart? Of course everyone will say I want to be beautiful inside out. This path is clear and it requires us to pass by this mortal earth by strict obedience to the Teachings of God.

> *Love seizeth not upon a living soul,*
> *The falcon preyeth not on a dead mouse.*

In the original language they have two words for "living soul", one word is "jan" which means a living spiritual soul and the other is "nafs" which is a living materialistic selfish soul. The word is nafs. The falcon of heaven wants us to be alive and living spiritually.

> *Love setteth a world aflame at every turn, and he wasteth every land where he carrieth his banner. Being hath no existence in his kingdom; the wise wield no command within his realm. The leviathan of love swalloweth the master of reason and destroyeth the*

lord of knowledge. He drinketh the seven seas, but his heart's thirst is still unquenched, and he saith, "Is there yet any more?" He shunneth himself and draweth away from all on earth.

> Love's a stranger to earth and heaven too;
> In him are lunacies seventy-and-two.

He hath bound a myriad victims in his fetters, wounded a myriad wise men with his arrow. Know that every redness in the world is from his anger, and every paleness in men's cheeks is from his poison. He yieldeth no remedy but death, he walketh not save in the valley of the shadow; yet sweeter than honey is his venom on the lover's lips, and fairer his destruction in the seeker's eyes than a hundred thousand lives.

This section of the valley of love gives us a graphic picture of this love being madness. Every war, prejudice, hate and strife is based on misguided love. If we have love without knowledge we act without sense or direction. Lovers all down through history have committed murder and self-destruction in suicides.

> Wherefore must the veils of the satanic self be burned away at the fire of love, that the spirit may be purified and cleansed and thus may know the station of the Lord of the Worlds.

> Kindle the fire of love and burn away all things,
> Then set thy foot into the land of the lovers.

The meaning of Satan has been misunderstood as meaning some creature with horns and a tail that sometimes takes on the form of a man and goes around corrupting people and leading them into hell or everlasting fire. Here Bahá'u'lláh gives us a clear explanation of Satan, that is the satanic self, the corrupt, greedy and selfish me. This Satan is always with me and here it tells us that in this all-consuming love of God these veils of my satanic self must be burned away. So the purpose of the valley of love is clearly stated.

And if, confirmed by the Creator, the lover escapes from the claws of the eagle of love, he will enter

THE VALLEY OF KNOWLEDGE

and come out of doubt into certitude, and turn from the darkness of illusion to the guiding light of the fear of God. His inner eyes will open and he will privily converse with his Beloved; he will set ajar the gate of truth and piety, and shut the doors of vain imaginings. He in this station is content with the decree of God, and seeth war as peace, and findeth in death the secrets of everlasting life. With inward and outward eyes he witnesseth the mysteries of resurrection in the realms of creation and the souls of men, and with a pure heart apprehendeth the divine wisdom in the endless Manifestations of God. In the ocean he findeth a drop, in a drop he beholdeth the secrets of the sea.

We are assured of God's confirmation for He has told us that if we make an effort He will guide us. If we are in motion aid from the invisible realm will be guiding us. Love is likened to an eagle that once we are captured by it, it holds us firmly. Then with the help of God we are set free. As we go from valley to valley it must be understood that these valleys are progressive, which means that as one passes out of the valley of search he does not stop searching but finding the beloved one the seeker searches for the way to get close and understand and commune with the beloved. Likewise, when we pass from the valley of love into the valley of knowledge our love increases and becomes knowledgeable. Without knowledge love alone would make us fanatics.

Everyone was born with eyes to see but all lived in a big house with many rooms and the house was in pitch blackness. So in truth it was as if everyone in the house was born blind. One day a man comes into the house and tells everyone in the house about sunshine. Of course, no one believes him. How can you explain about sunshine in a pitch black house to a people who for all intents and purposes are blind. The task is indeed a formidable one. This is exactly the situation of those unique and wonderful spiritual Teachers that from time to time and age to age come into this world to teach us spiritual truths.

This man in the pitch black darkness of the house gets a few people that are willing to listen and he takes each of them by the hand and say, "Now feel how warm my hand is, Well, sunshine is warm like that, but ever so much warmer." Then he picks up a stick and gives each person a good clout on the head and says, "See those stars, that's light, but ever so much brighter, and it is not only for the moment that you receive the clout. In fact, you don't even have to get a clout." This great and wonderful teacher uses everything he can in that dark house to teach the people about sunshine.

A few people in that dark house are still doubtful most do not believe him at all. The doubtful ones think just maybe he might be right. They are the people with faith and they ask for directions to get outside and experience this glorious sunshine. The teacher very carefully and exactly gives the directions. Most people only follow the directions that are easy and in accord with their desires, of course, they can't find the door. Some others try sincerely but do not pay close attention to the instructions so must make repeated attempts. However, there are always a few who will follow the instructions exactly and they come to the door and step out into the dazzling brilliance of the sun. This is certitude. The one that has left the dark house of disbelief and stepped into the brilliant sunshine of truth. He will never go back into that dark house and say, "I believe the sun is shining." This enlightened one, goes back, and says. "I know the sun is shining."

This Valley of Knowledge takes us out of the dark house of doubt and brings us into the full sunshine of certitude. In the Valley of Search we rode on the steed of patience and in the Valley of Love we rode on the steed of pain; in the Valley of Knowledge we need a guiding light and that guiding light is "the fear of God".

Bahá'u'lláh explains that when one is in the Valley of Knowledge that one is content with the decree of God and in the beginning he knows the end will be God's will.

When one reaches the valley of knowledge Bahá'u'lláh teaches us that the one in this valley sees the end in the beginning. The one who knows has given up his own will and follows only the will of God. Such a person "is content with the decree of God".

In 1953 I was doing research for the United States government in computers when the call came from the Bahá'í World Center with the need for some of us to arise and go to the remotest parts of the earth. I had a wife and one baby four years old, one baby two years old and one only three weeks old. I quit my job and with my family moved to the Aleutian Islands. My goal was the Island of Unalaska which is about eight hundred miles from Anchorage, Alaska in the middle of the Bering Sea.

The Bahá'ís are not supported and must work. We also must try to help with what we call "Social and Economic Development Programs". Unalaska had about fifty families of native Aleut people. Many of the children were malnourished, suffered from rickets and there was no work. The houses were not insulated and the people used drift wood from the beach and coal that the military had buried after World War II, to heat their poor houses. Of course there was no work for a scientist, so I became a fisherman.

With a hand seamer, a pressure cooker and a twelve foot boat I put up 42 cases of salmon. Each case was 48 one pound cans. I could not hire any help and I did electronic repair work and became the United States postmaster for my income.

In ten years time the cannery had grown from our original 42 cases per year to a capacity of about, 100,000 cases per year, with an operational season year-around instead of only two months in the summer. Our main product had gone from salmon to the world-famous King Crab. We were also putting up about 500 tons of frozen King Crab.

A restlessness began to creep into my soul at this time. I felt that we had done all we could for the Aleutian Islands. The people all had work now, they heated their homes with oil and had insulated their houses and everyone had electricity and some even had cars and trucks and the children were well fed and healthy. However, my roots had gone down so deeply that it seemed impossible to break free... like the heavenly bird described by Bahá'u'lláh, which soars on the wings of detachment and nearness to God, then descends into the mire and clay to satisfy its hunger, and with sullied wings is unable to resume its flight. I never had any purpose save service to God and humanity in this, our pioneering post, and never in the entire ten years had I let slip that pioneering spirit—first must come the Cause of God—that dominated our lives. Then it happened.

Everything was running very smoothly, although in a business such as we were in, one was always in debt. For example, we would can $100,000 worth of crab, ship it to Seattle, and upon presentation of warehouse receipts would receive $70,000 advance on the future sale of the product. Eventually we would, after sale and costs, receive the additional $30,000 or whatever was left. Shortly after one such shipment, however, instead of a check we received word that the bank had refused the advance. To iron out the difficulties, I kissed my family goodbye, closed the cannery, and left for Seattle, descending into that black and ruinous pit Bahá'u'lláh so vividly describes. In Seattle I went to my banker whom I had done business with for over ten years. He informed me that the multi-million dollar canning company had informed them that they must choose. They could do business with us or with them. I had taken away some of their best customers with a better product and at a cheaper price. I concluded that as I owed over $30,000 to my fishermen alone, it would be best to sell at cost and clear out. Again the competition was ahead of me and had just put 100,000 cases of crab on the market at $50 under cost. Of course, all these companies had to do was raise the price of their fruit or vegetables a few pennies a case to recoup their loss on the crab. But alas, for us, we had only the crab, and faced bankruptcy.

At night I would go to bed and instead of a heart burning with the love of God, it was one filled with those sordid and worthless problems of life, and in the morning instead of "I have wakened in Thy shelter, Oh my God", it was "Oh God, how can I pay my fisherman?" I could lock the cannery door and leave, except that I had tremendous responsibilities to others. I had planned to be gone a week and it now stretched out into six months. I had a real glimpse of the reality of hell, and only an infinitely merciful God could deliver me from its flame. Totally immersed in the muck of materialism, I was swept into the vortex of a raging river like a small chip of wood. As it drew to the time of the Bahá'í ninteen Day Fast I decided I was doing no good in Seattle, and since the Fast was a very special family time, I returned to my island. As the Winter of Desolation must give way to the reality and warmth of the new Spring, so the spirit of God began to revive my drooping soul, as I turned to the healing waters of obedience to God. I am sure that only His tender love and compassion could have lifted me out of this slough of heedlessness.

As the Fast progressed, I began slowly, and then more rapidly, advancing once more into that realm of God from which I had descended. One day, while at complete peace and contentment, the revelation was born upon my spirit, "God doeth whatsoever He willeth". Oh, what joy and relief permeated my being! My actions had been those of someone trying to play God. Oh God! My God, have mercy upon me! God is All-Knowing and All-Wise. In His infinite wisdom He decided whether these children must return to their former state of poverty for their own best interest. Possibly this poverty would allow us to leave and go forward on the Nine Year Plan. Was not my primary concern due to a tender love for these Aleut people? In any event God doeth whatsoever He willeth; all are His servants and all abide by His bidding.

After Naw-Rúz (Bahá'í New Year) that year, I left home for Seattle again, completely submerged in the inner reality of these thoughts. I was repeating to myself over and over again, "I am content with the Will of God". Upon my arrival in Seattle, I did not contact the banks, brokers or wholesalers but instead called my Bahá'í friends and offered them my services for the weekend. On Friday I spoke at the Seattle Bahá'í Center and the meeting was indeed a heavenly one.

Upon returning to my hotel that night, the people were all gathered around the TV and the news of the great Alaskan earthquake of Good Friday 1964 was being announced on television, with a magnitude of 8.6 on the Richter Scale. The reports stated that the Aleutian Islands had ceased to exist. I walked over to the elevator and as I pushed the button for my floor I caught myself saying, "I am cont...", I stopped and asked myself the question, "Jenabe are you really content with the Will of God". My most precious family was alone on one of those tiny islands. I went into my room and sat on the bed and had one of my most deep soul examinations of my life. The result was complete contentment with God's Will and Pleasure, followed by a soul-stirring prayer for my family's protection and advancement, whether still in this world or in the next kingdom. Of course, as it turned out, the radio and television announcements were greatly exaggerated, and the islands were completely untouched. My wife had loaded many of the townspeople into our company's bus and driven them to the hills; but people decided that they would rather drown in the tidal wave than freeze to death on the mountain, and had returned to their homes.

This great earthquake lasted only three mintues, but in that three minutes every problem we had was completely solved. The company which was intent upon our destruction lost every canning plant they had in Alaska. On Monday the brokers and wholesalers fell over themselves to purchase my pack at full price. Another company that had lost their plant contacted me and arrangements were made to lease to them our business, thus freeing me for further service to the Cause of God and insuring my beloved Aleuts of continued employment. Within the week, I was returning to Unalaska for my family. Since that time my business was sold and the money was spent in doing Bahá'í work in 62 countries.

In this valley of knowledge one starts to understand the promise of God to never leave mankind without help and knows that these Teachers from God always came in the past, come in the present and will continue to come in the future.

> *Split the atom's heart, and lo!*
> *Within it thou wilt find a sun.*

It is interesting to note that Bahá'u'lláh wrote this over one hundred years ago. Now we have split the atoms heart and found the sun of atomic and hydrogen power.

> *The wayfarer in this Valley seeth in the fashionings of the True One nothing save clear providence, and at every moment saith: "No defect canst thou see in the creation of the God of Mercy: Repeat the gaze: Seest thou a single flaw?" He beholdeth justice in injustice, and in justice, grace. In ignorance he findeth many a knowledge hidden, and in knowledge a myriad wisdoms manifest. He breaketh the cage of the body and the passions, and consorteth with the people of the immortal realm. He mounteth on the ladders of inner truth and hasteneth to the heaven of inner*

significance. He rideth in the ark of "we shall show them our signs in the regions and in themselves", and journeyeth over the sea of "until it become plain to them that (this Book) is the truth". And if he meeteth with injustice he shall have patience, and if he cometh upon wrath he shall manifest love.

The wayfarer in the valley of knowledge, knows that God's work is perfect and the defects one sees are the results of man's doings. Again Bahá'u'lláh assures us although one may suffer from injustice the end result will be a true justice because mankind learns best through experience. He teaches us to be patient and loving even during dire difficulties for the final end will be God's ultimate purpose for mankind.

This next story written by Bahá'u'lláh about the lover gives us a beautiful example of the valley of search, the valley of love and in the end the valley of knowledge.

There was once a lover who had sighed for long years in separation from his beloved, and wasted in the fire of remoteness. From the rule of love, his heart was empty of patience, and his body weary of his spirit; he reckoned life without her as a mockery, and time consumed him away. How many a day he found no rest in longing for her; how many a night the pain of her kept him from sleep; his body was worn to a sigh, his heart's wound had turned him to a cry of sorrow. He had given a thousand lives for one taste of the cup of her presence, but it availed him not. The doctors knew no cure for him, and companions avoided his company; yea, physicians have no medicine for one sick of love, unless the favor of the beloved one deliver him.

At last, the tree of his longing yielded the fruit of despair, and the fire of his hope fell to ashes. Then one night he could live no more, and he went out of his house and made for the marketplace. On a sudden, a watchman followed after him. He broke into a run, with the watchman following; then other watchmen came together, and barred every passage to the weary one. And the wretched one cried from his heart, and ran here and there, and moaned to himself: "Surely this watchman is Izrá'íl, my angel of death, following so fast upon me; or he is a tyrant of men, seeking to harm me". His feet carried him on, the one bleeding with the arrow of love, and his heart lamented. Then he came to a garden wall, and with untold pain he scaled it, for it proved very high; and forgetting his life, he threw himself down to the garden.

And there he beheld his beloved with a lamp in her hand, searching for a ring she had lost. When the heart-surrendered lover looked on his ravishing love, he drew a great breath and raised up his hands in prayer, crying: "O God! Give Thou glory to the watchman, and riches and long life. For the watchman was Gabriel, guiding this poor one; or he was Isráfíl, bringing life to this wretched one!"

Indeed, his words were true, for he had found many a secret justice in this seeming tyranny of the watchman, and seen how many a mercy lay hid behind the veil. Out of wrath, the guard had led him who was athirst in love's desert to the sea of his loved one, and lit up the dark night of absence with the light of reunion. He had driven one who was afar, into the garden of nearness, had guided an ailing soul to the heart's physician.

Now if the lover could have looked ahead, he would have blessed the watchman at the start, and prayed on his behalf, and he would have seen that tyranny as justice; but since the end was veiled to him, he moaned and made his plaint in the beginning. Yet those who journey in the garden land of knowledge, because they see the end in the beginning, see peace in war and friendliness in anger.

There was no help for this lover as long as he sat in his house. He finally left his house and headed for the market which could mean his goal was now material. As he was in motion God's help moved him back to his spiritual goal which he achieved by climbing the wall of self, and forgetting even his life he threw himself from the wall and arrived at the feet of his loved one. Another interesting point that can be made is that in this day Bahá'u'lláh shining with the light of God is searching for this ring of unity which has been lost by mankind. Bahá'u'lláh tells us that if a jewel lies hidden beyond the seven seas and buried under a mountain He will in this day find it and bring it to light.

I had a personal experience myself of this mysterious way in which Bahá'u'lláh will find these hidden jewels. I was teaching in Mexico around 1966. One day when I got up I told another Bahá'í that was with me that we were going to Taviche.

"Where is Taviche?" this teacher asked.

"I don't know I've never heard of it," I replied.

We checked the map, and sure enough, there was a village named Taviche and it was at the end of a small narrow gauge train track. We were delighted to be able to ride on a train for a change instead of driving or hiking, which was the norm. On the train into Taviche we tried unsuccessfully to talk to the people. When the train finally arrived at the end of the line there was only a train station and no village. I asked the train conductor where Taviche was and he said it was about half a kilometer up the trail. I explained that we wanted to go to Taviche and he said, "Go ahead".

"But," I replied, "I also want to go back to the city on the train".

The conductor laughed and said, "Well, I'm sorry but you can't do both. The train turns around here and in 10 minutes will return to the city". He further explained that there was no place to stay in the village, and that the only way out, other than by train, was to hike across the desert to the highway and catch the bus. This trek was over 10 miles.

Reason and common sense now took hold and in my mind I wrote off Taviche, and went off to play with some children that had come to meet the train. The other Bahá'í teacher stayed and talked to this conductor. Later on in the train my companion said, "Do you know what that conductor said to me? He told me no one in the whole world cares anything about the people that live in Taviche".

This remark went right to my heart, and I declared that on the following day we would return to Taviche, with proper big sombreros or hats and plenty of water, we would tell the people that there were people all over the world that loved them and cared about them. Then we would make our trek to the highway across the desert.

The next morning, with my sons to help carry the lunch and water and with the other Bahá'í teacher, we were on the train once again for Taviche. We waved good-by to the conductor and set off up the trail to Taviche. The feeling I had was that someone was pulling me up that trail. When we rounded a bend in the trail, Taviche came into view. It was on the side of a hill. My friend said, "Let's go up the hill and visit the houses and work our way down and out of the village".

"No", I said.

"OK", she replied. "Let's start up the hill and visit all the houses and then come down and out of the village".

"No", I again answered her. "We are going to that house right up there". Which we proceeded to do. When we knocked on the door a beautiful young man opened the door and lovingly invited us in and told us to sit down.

"Why have you come here?" he said.

"For God", I replied.

"Listen to me", he interrupted. "I'm going to tell you why you have come. Last night in my dream, you two foreigners came to me and told me that you were coming to bring me a new message from God. I stayed home and cleaned my house and waited for you to come". Now, although the Bahá'í teacher with me came from Venezuela, she was dark-skinned, with black hair, black eyes and looked like any other Mexican. Up to this time she had not said a single word, yet this man used the word foreigners. His name was Efraen Hernandez de Perez. He had graduated from the University and had returned to that village because he wanted to help his people.

This man most enthusiastically accepted the Cause and wanted something to read. Because we knew we would have to hike through the desert we had tried to keep our load down, so had not brought any Books with us. We then proceeded up the mountain, and never had we been met with such animosity. When we tried to speak to the people they would actually spit and turn away. The other teacher offered a woman a pamphlet and this woman snatched the tract out of the teacher's hand, tore it up and threw it on the ground.

We returned to Efraen and explained that we had so many villages, and so many Bahá'ís that were eager and hungry for the heavenly table, that we felt compelled to leave Taviche. This precious soul pleaded that at least we must bring him some books, which we promised to do but set no time. We then hiked out through the desert to the highway and back to the city. So it was about six months later, after I had bought a 4-wheel drive all terrain vehicle, that I drove across the desert to see Efraen in Taviche. He was not at home, so we left the books and promised to return the first Sunday two months away. We asked his wife to tell him to expect us, barring some unforeseen problem, we would surely come.

The story of this young man spread across Mexico and several Bahá'ís, including the Continental Counsellor in Mexico at that time, accompanied us on this planned visit to meet such an outstanding Bahá'í. As planned, we arrived in Taviche and when we inquired for Efraen were advised that he was dead. I was amazed and said, "But he is a young man and two months ago was out working in his field when we came".

"He's dead", was the reply. "The whole family is putting the marker on his grave today".

We went to Efraen's mother's house and there were around 15 adults and a number of children were present.

The sadness was over powering and we all went to work to help ease this grieving family through their ordeal. I talked to the mother, held her hand and explained about life after death and God, like a loving gardener transplanting her son from a dark and gloomy world into a world of light. The grief was still there but it was no longer as oppressive and the mother said, "I want to tell you all how my son died". So I called over the Counsellor and the other Bahá'ís all gathered around. The Counsellor was a native of Mexico and a native speaker so there can be no doubt about this story.

"I heard that my son was sick", she said. "So I went to see him. He had a slight fever. He told me that he tried to tell the people of Taviche about Bahá'í but no one would listen. So he decided that he would give his life so that the people of Taviche would learn and accept the Cause of God. I cried out, 'No! No! let me go get the priest.' My son looked at me very sternly and said, "Mother, mother please don't take me away from my God". In three days this young man was dead. We then went with the family to the grave site for prayers. Because we were on the edge of the desert the weather was extremely hot, but the Counsellor, who was wearing a sleeveless blouse, had goose bumps on her arms from the special spiritual atmosphere at that grave-side. We then went back to the mother's house where Efraen's wife was waiting for us with the Bahá'í Books we had left two months before. On the fly-leaf of each well-used Book Efraen had written, "Praise be to God, the Lord of Eternity". He had signed his name and dated the books. That day the whole family became Bahá'ís, so we had 15 wonderful new friends in Taviche. Within six months the whole village was transformed and when I would drive into the village, the people would hear my truck and rush out and plead with me to come to their house that day and talk about God with them.

As Bahá'u'lláh wrote in this Valley of Knowledge He, "had guided an ailing soul to the heart's physician". If I had been truly in the Valley of Knowledge I would have known in the beginning that the end would further God's cause.

> *Such is the state of the wayfarers in this Valley; but the people of the Valleys above this see the end and the beginning as one; nay, they see neither beginning nor end, and witness neither "first" nor "last". Nay rather, the denizens of the undying city, who dwell in the green garden land, see not even "neither first nor last"; they fly from all that is first, and repulse all that is last.*
>
> *For these have passed over the worlds of names, and fled beyond the worlds of attributes as swift as lightning. Thus is it said: "Absolute Unity excludeth all attributes". And they have made their dwelling-place in the shadow of the Essence.*

In this passage we were being prepared for the higher valleys. Where in the valley of knowledge we could see the end in the beginning, in the higher valleys there is neither a beginning nor an end. An example of going beyond names and attributes is the sun. The attributes of the sun are light, heat, energy, and various types of rays. If we can close our eyes to these names and attributes all that is there is the sun.

> *Wherefore, relevant to this, Khájih Ábdu'lláh—may God the Most High sanctify his beloved spirit—hath made a subtle point and spoken an eloquent word as to the meaning of "Guide Thou us on the straight path", which is: "Show us the right way, that is, honor us with the love of Thine Essence, that we may be freed from turning toward ourselves and toward all else save Thee, and may become wholly Thine, and know only Thee, and see only Thee, and think of none save Thee."*
>
> *Nay, these even mount above this station, wherefore it is said:*
> *Love is a veil betwixt the lover and the loved one;*
> *More than this I am not permitted to tell.*

Let's take a journey into space. As we stand on the beach we can see the sand around us. As we go up we no longer can see the grains of sand but we see the whole beach. Higher up we no longer see the beach we see the continent. Higher still we see the planet, then the solar system then the galaxy, then the galaxies and finally we see the whole creation. The person that goes into these higher valleys only sees the Creator.

The little verse states that as love is one of the attributes of God it can be a veil.

At this hour the morn of knowledge hath arisen and the lamps of wayfaring and wandering are quenched.

When the sun comes up one no longer needs a lamp and when the light of God is lit in His Manifestation we should be able to see Him clearly.

Veiled from this way Moses
Though all strength and light;
Then thou who hast no wings at all,
Attempt not flight.

Moses wandered forty years in the desert searching for the promised land. Then He was not allowed to enter. So it is as if Moses was the Messenger for the Valley of Search. Then Christ came and the core or most fundamental teaching was love. Christ was the Messenger for the Valley of Love. Then Muhammad came as the Messenger for the Valley of Knowledge. His most fundamental teaching was knowledge and from His Teachings the first Universities were built. Now Bahá'u'lláh has come as the Messenger for the Valley of Unity. The center and fundamental truth of His message is unity. Peace on earth and the unity of all peoples and nations.

Where in the Valley of Search and Knowledge we needed the horses and in the Valley of Knowledge we need the lamp, now in the Valley of Unity we need wings. These wings are wings of the spirit with which we can fly into the Teachings of God. We are given our wings from the Manifestations of God, who will help us.

The sea is the sea of Divine Reality, the sea of existence, the sea of God. This ocean is preexistent. It is eternal in the past, eternal in the future and imperishable. Although it is of

The Seven Valleys of Bahá'u'lláh

God, it is not God. God is and ever will be that Supreme Unknowable Essence, the Creator of all that is and all that will ever be. This sea can only be understood or comprehended in light of those unique and wondrous souls that appear from time to time and age to age in the form of human beings, but divine in origin. The sea is Christ for the Christian, Moses for the Jew, Muhammad for the Moslem, Krishna for the Hindu and so on. The true believer in the Oneness of God knows that all these enlightened Teachers speak the same truth. They show forth the same divine qualities and are the bearers of the same message. In reality the ocean is one and the teacher is one. To be in the presence of these Holy Souls is to be in the presence of God or as near to God as man can ever get. To be in their ocean is to be in the ocean of God.

The ocean surges, the tides move in the endless cycles. There is motion and in this motion stillness is found. The ocean of God is one yet it is composed of uncountable drops. Remove the drops and the ocean would cease to exist. The ocean is contained in the sea bed and yet it surrounds and can not be contained.

The winds, waves and currents that seem to us random and aimless and without purpose are in truth created and moved in accordance with a divine will and purpose far beyond our limited understanding. For example, the wind of the Will of God blows across the surface of the sea and a tiny drop is selected and carried aloft. Borne by this divine wind it is carried far and high over the mountain, it is released and falls to earth as rain. At the moment of contact with the earth, it is the moment of conception and an individual soul comes into existence. A Mozart, an Einstein, a Gandhi, a peasant, a pauper all are born into the world of material being. There is no choice on our part as to where and when we are born. All are created from the same spiritual water out of the same Divine Sea, but in accordance with the divine will and purpose as to the where and when.

What and where is the destiny of the drop? Back to the sea of course. One and all we flow back down to the sea. As the drop proceeds over the earth of material existence it picks up and carries along with itself the dirt and filth it accumulates during its earthly travels. Now there is a difference however as the drop has a certain degree of free will. It is true that it is pulled by the forces of gravity and it must and it will return to the sea. The drop must go over the waterfalls where it is to be cleaned and oxygenated. It is beaten on the rocks of life. It must traverse the rapids put in its path by providence. Yet that element of free will is also found in the river. The drop comes to a fork in the river and the God sent teacher tries to teach the little drop about right, wrong, truth, falsehood, virtue, honour and morality. He pleads with the drop to take the right fork and the safe path to God but the current created by the majority of the drops going left and away from God tries to pull him in their direction. The drop must fight against the current and go right but it can only succeed if it wants to.

This is the only free will mankind has. The purpose of life on this plane is to know and to love God. To know God is to know His Teacher and to love God is to love His Teacher and to love our fellow man. This requires free will. Love to be true love must be freely given with no compulsion, no force. One loves because one wants to not because one has to. If love is forced it is not love at all. The true lover, loves his beloved with no thought of receiving something in return. The true lover says, "What can I do for you? How can I make you happy?" not, "What can you do for me? How can you make me happy?" The Creator's love is this kind of pure love even for the least of His creation. It is shown by the life giving sunshine, the life sustaining rain, pure air and bounties without limit for all. What the Creator wants for man is for man's sake, not for God's sake. He is the All-Knowing, the All-Wise, the Omnipotent, the Omnipresent and as such He knows what is best for the creature he has created and loves. Through His teacher and His guidance He points us in the right direction for our own eternal happiness. If we

The Seven Valleys of Bahá'u'lláh

in turn return that love we will do what He wants us to do to the very best of our ability.

As the drop continues its journey to the sea it is very important that through its free will it seeks association and contact with and flows down river with drops that are also trying to love their Creator. If it flows with sewage, it will become sewage. Of course it can then go through the waste water treatment plant and be cleansed of the sewage but this cleaning is a very difficult operation. For example, if one has a glass of pure water and only one drop of ink is added, the whole glass is soiled by the ink and it is very difficult to clean. Sometimes, in fact, the only way the drop can be cleansed again is to go through the agony of extreme suffering. The drop must be boiled at very high temperature, turned to steam, condensed and then returned to its stream of life, where the drop will wend its way onward to the sea.

Finally, the drop comes to the river's mouth. If it is clean and pure, it can flow unhindered back into the sea. If not it is washed back and forth by the tides and surf until all the silt of self is deposited and left behind on the delta of the river. The big difference between the drop that came out of the sea and the drop that returns to the sea is that the returning drop now possesses individuality. From here to eternity that individual soul will continue to exist as you or me. WE ALL COME FROM GOD AND TO GOD WE WILL RETURN.

After passing through the Valley of Knowledge, which is the last plane of limitation,

The first three valleys are limited valleys and this Valley of Unity is unlimited. Some are not even in the valleys and they don't receive any light. Some are in the valley of search, others in the Valley of Love, and others in the Valley of Knowledge so they will only see the limited light from their own vantage point of limitations. The one who is truly in this Valley of Unity will see only the light with unlimited vision. The wayfarer in this valley will be immersed in an ocean of oneness.

the wayfarer cometh to

THE VALLEY OF UNITY

and drinketh from the cup of the Absolute, and gazeth on the Manifestations of Oneness. In this station he pierceth the veils of plurality, fleeth from the worlds of the flesh, and ascendeth into the heaven of singleness. With the ear of God he heareth, with the eye of God he beholdeth the mysteries of divine creation. He steppeth into the sanctuary of the Friend, and shareth as an intimate the pavilion of the Loved One. He stretcheth out the hand of truth from the sleeve of the Absolute; he revealeth the secrets of power. He seeth in himself neither name nor fame nor rank, but findeth his own praise in praising God. He beholdeth in his own name the name of God; to him, "all songs are from the King", and every melody from Him. He sitteth on the throne of "Say, all is from God", and taketh his rest on the carpet of "There is no power or might but in God". He looketh on all things with the eye of oneness, and seeth the brilliant rays of the divine sun shining from the dawning-point of Essence alike on all created things, and the lights of singleness reflected over all creation.

In the Valley of Unity the wayfarer does not want a name, fame nor rank. All songs are from the king. I will use another analogy to help us understand this point of self-sacrifice.

The stirring of consciousness was a very slow process for the sailor. It seemed that from the beginning of time for him there had been many other ships and many other sailors on the sea, all telling him what to do, where to go and even helping him to take care of his ship or taking care of it for him. These sailors were named mother, father, brother, sister, aunt, uncle, teacher and even friend. With this dawning of this consciousness, slowly but surely, came the realization that all these other sailors had no real idea about why they were on this ocean or where they were

The Seven Valleys of Bahá'u'lláh

supposed to be going. They knew a great deal about their own ship, and how to keep it going, but had little or no real knowledge of the sailor aboard the ship.

With the dawning of true self-consciousness came a longing desire to know. The sailor wanted answers to the questions: Why am I here? What is my purpose? Where am I supposed to be going? Where is port? Is there even a port? A deep seated reason began to exert itself telling the sailor that if this ocean was all there was, life was empty and meaningless. To come upon this ocean, spend your days like water running out of a bathtub, wandering in pursuit of momentary pleasures, then the whole journey was a farce. Another deep seated conviction reasoned that this perfectly organized and most beautiful creation had a purpose, a master plan, a safe harbor and a home port. All one had to do was to find these answers, which must be out there, and all would be meaningful and clear.

So the sailor started out on his quest. His first goal was a very logical one, EDUCATION. He told himself that he would surely find his answers there. The sailor, looked out across the ocean, in the distance he was sure he saw something real. So he strove with all his might to reach it, in the end it was only mist on the sea. Yes, over there was something he had missed, surely that was the problem. This time it was nothing more than seaweed. So with all his might and main he chased the false god of education, from glittering on the waves to mists rising from the water. In the end he was disillusioned and heartsick. The education he had attained was not an answer, it only raised more questions. This education was not about life and living, but the method to acquire material possessions that in the end would be left upon the sea.

So the sailor decided that surely the purpose must be in acquiring those very possessions. From the false god of education, he had learned much about how to secure them. Once again he set sail for what he thought would be the secure harbor of "fortune", in the end he was to find it also empty, void and meaningless in the passage across the ocean of life. In his pursuit of material things, he had been careless of other's ships, leaving many a ship floundering in his wake.

Now, the sailor had eliminated education and fortune, and he found that they did not bring the sought for answers. His next direction was fame. At least if he became famous, he thought, his name would be remembered on the sea of life by other ships and other sailors in the future. This ego trip ended in the same unhappy way as the chasing of all the other false gods. He did not find his purpose or the purpose of life in the god of education, god of marriage, god of family, god of fortune, or the god of fame. These were all useful while sailing upon the sea. When viewed in the proper sequence of time they were no more than a flash of consciousness in the cosmos. To live and to die, so what?

The sailor is carried along by every current, pushed by every changing wind, and drifting first in one direction today, and back the way he came tomorrow. His movement seems to be aimless and apparently fruitless upon the ocean of life. It appears, what many suspect, there is no purpose to life, only chance.

The sailor, dejected, depressed, hopeless and helpless reached deep within his anguished soul. He brought forth an unconscious and unspoken prayer, but one deeply felt, "O! God, please help me".

One day, the sailor meets another ship and talks to another sailor. This seemingly chance meeting will change the sailor's life forever. His heartfelt prayer has been answered.

The new found friend tells the sailor about a great and wonderful Captain, an all knowing and all wise Captain. He knows the ocean. He is an expert navigator. He even knows where we are supposed to be going and how to get there. The greatest news of all however, is that His prime purpose and main objective is to help every one that wants the help to arrive safely to home port.

"Where can this marvelous Captain be found and how does one get in contact with Him", the sailor asks. "Will He

The Seven Valleys of Bahá'u'lláh   51

come, really come aboard my ship and truly see me into safe harbor?"

"The Captain is near, very near, nearer than your very breath and life, He can be contacted through your radio[1] and yes, He will come aboard your ship. He will see you safely to home port", replies the friend, and he sails away into the ocean's dreamlike mists. In fact, although the sailor knows he was awake it all seemed like a wonderful dream.

The sailor in a frenzy rushes into the radio room and begins turning on switches. He has never used the radio before. He shouts into the microphone, "<u>SOS SOS SOS</u>. <u>S</u>ave <u>O</u>ur <u>S</u>oul". All he gets from the radio is static. Unless one very carefully tunes the radio, all he will ever get is static. The sailor tries everything he can think of, still all that comes through is the crackling of static. Finally, when everything else had failed, he decided to read the instructions.[2] When everything else fails, read the instructions. Now, following the instructions very carefully, what the Book says to do he does. What the Book says don't do he doesn't do. Soon he gets right on the station and his radio is very fine tuned.

"Captain, hello Captain, this is sailor, on unknown sea, in unknown ship, calling the Captain. Do you read me Captain, please come in. Over". He calls on the radio.

"Hello sailor this is the Captain I read you loud and clear. You are sailing the ship of creation on the ocean of life. Can I help you?" A voice comes through the speakers loud and clear.

The sailor is momentarily dumbfounded. He never really expected anyone to answer. He was sure that this would also prove to be just one more frustration and another of life's disappointments, added to all the others, he had so far endured. When he recovered from his surprise he replied, "Captain this is sailor. Is it true that you can navigate? You know your way across the ocean? You

---

[1] Prayer, Supplication and Meditation.
[2] The Holy books, the Torah, the Bible, the Koran, the Aqdas etc.

also know where port is? Will you come aboard my ship and help me?"

"Yes, it is true I have that knowledge", replied the Captain. "Yes, I will come aboard your ship and see you safely into home port. However, there are some conditions: First, you must clean up that ship. Your heart is the place where I will reside, it must be clean. Second, you must agree, I am the Captain and you are the sailor. Both of us can't be in command at the same time. You must turn yourself and your ship completely over to me. You must trust me and obey me explicitly. Do you agree to the conditions?"

"Oh yes, I do, I do, I agree", thrilled the sailor. "I will clean up the ship at once. Over and out".

The sailor went out on deck, his ship was indeed in a mess. Garbage was everywhere. The lines were all tangled up. The brass had all turned green. The paint, long ago, had turned to rust. The lights had gone out. The engines were sputtering and missing. Yet, the sailor turned to with a will, his desire and purpose were great.

He attacked the garbage strewn deck. He picked up an old rusty tin can, held it fondly and said to himself, "My mother taught me this surely it is valuable". So he set it aside. Then it was the broken bottle that he had learned in the university. The old piece of string his friend had given to him. The tattered torn rags of a lost and almost forgotten love. The results of his deck cleaning was to just rearrange all the garbage. He disposed of only a small and insignificant amount of his trash. He then tackled the tangled lines of his life and they seemed to be so hopelessly entwined he was sure they could not be untangled. So he opend a hatch and stuffed these lines into the hold. As for the rust, he got some paint and painted over it.

Of course the sailor is not at fault in his attempt to clean up his ship. The truth is, he just did not know how. How could he possibly distinguish truth from falsehood, good from bad, or right from wrong? The point is that he did his best. He really tried.

The sailor rushed to his radio and happily advised the Captain that the ship was all cleaned up and ready for the Captain to come aboard. Now, this Captain is most loving, most kind and most understanding. He knew that the sailor had done his best, so he told the sailor to pipe him aboard. He again warned the sailor to remember that He is the Captain and the sailor is only the sailor, both of them can not command the ship.

"Aye, aye sir. I fully understand. You are the Captain and I am sailor. Standing by for orders, sir".

"All right sailor let's really clean up the ship. We will start with truth and truthfulness", responded the Captain.

"I'm sorry sir but I don't understand the order. You mean for me to be true to you, true to others and even true to muself?" said the sailor.

"That's exactly right", the Captain advised. "I know you don't understand, but just carry on, do the best you can and the understanding will come as you put the orders into practice".

Now the sailor with renewed dedication, disposes of all the garbage and junk. The sailor tries to follow the orders. Such orders as to be kind, be loving, be gentle, be sweet, be giving, be forgiving, be faithful, be honest, be pure hearted, be humble and think more of others than you think of yourself. The commands of the Captain come and the sailor puts forth all his effort to obey. Soon the decks are cleared, the tangled lines all neatly coiled in their proper places, the brass like golden mirrors gleams in the sun, the deck is spotless, the rust removed and new paint put on, the lights all burn brightly and the engines purr like kittens. The ship now moves across the ocean of life with meaning and purpose and true direction. The white wake trails off behind the moving vessel like a white pathway to heaven. The sailor is elated, excited and delighted. He has become a new sailor with a new ship. The sailor with a song in his heart says, "Oh Captain, my Captain, I love you so, I love you so, beloved".

"Oh yeah!" says the Captain. "Let's find out".

The hurricane hits the unsuspecting ship with undreamt of violence. The wind screams through the rigging, green water washing over her decks. She keels over and flounders in waves 30 feet high. The sailor is terrified. He rushes into the pilot house, pushes the Captain aside, and shouts, "We're sinking! We're sinking! Give me the Ship! Give me the ship!" In an instant, the Captain is gone. In the worst possible situation and at the worst possible time the sailor kicks his Captain off the ship. The truth of the matter is clear, the sailor did not really trust the Captain. Somehow the sailor manages to get through the storm. His ship veers off course. At first imperceptible, garbage again appears on deck, lights go out, paint peels, iron rusts, brass starts to turn green again, and the lines of his life start to once more become tangled. The sailor remembering how happy and wonderful it was with the Captain aboard finally, in desperation, goes back to his radio and tries to reach the Captain. All he gets from his pleading on the radio is silence. "They shall cry out for help and receive no answer". Helpless and hopeless he spends his days trying to get through to the Captain only to be met, day after day, by the total silence. At last he gives up in despair. Dejected, he has reached the depths of despair. He feels only death can now deliver him from his agony. Suddenly the radio comes to life and this ever loving, ever forgiving and most merciful Captain is there again reassuring the sailor. As every tide ebbs, it also floods.

"I'm sorry my Captain. Please forgive me. Please come back. I do love you. I will trust you", pleads the sailor.

"Alright sailor, but remember this is not a game or a trifle. This is the very serious business of life. You must trust me. You must put your faith wholly in me. You must give me complete command of your ship. Only then will I see you over the sea and into safe harbor. Once again, sailor. You must clean up that ship and then I will return to you".

This time the Captain does not come aboard until the ship is spotless, for He knows that the sailor now knows how to clean it. When the garbage strewn deck is spotless, the lines properly coiled, the engines humming, the brass gleaming, the Captain once more comes aboard. The sailor is truly grateful. He breaths a great sigh of relief and happiness. He vows that he will let the ship sink and be annihilated rather than again lose his Captain.

With the ship back on course the sailor responds with a willing and loving heart to the commands of the Captain. He begins to see with the eye of the Captain, hear with the ear of the Captain, and begins to understand with the heart of the Captain. He even begins to learn how to navigate the ship and has a dim and distant view of where port is and the safe harbor of home. The sailor once more with deeply felt emotion says, "I love you so my Captain, my beloved, my truth and my life".

Again the Captain responds with, "Oh, yeah, let's find out".

This time when the catastrophic hurricane hits, the waves are 60 feet high. The ship trembles and goes under green water with such violence that the sailor is sure it can never recover. He is terrified beyond belief, but he is more terrified of once again losing his Captain. Trembling all over with fear, in an ice cold sweat and almost dumb with terror, he finally stutters, "Orrrders susususu-sir".

"Steady as she goes, sailor", responds the Captain.

"Stu-stu-stu-steady, sh-sh-sh-she is sir", blurts out the sailor. It seems as if the sailor has never been so scared in his whole life. All of a sudden the storm is over, the wind dies down, the sun comes out and the waves subside. The sailor is elated. He tells himself, "That storm was twice as bad as the other one and yet, the Captain saw me through it so easily. I truly do trust my Captain. He is indeed the most wonderful Captain."

During the next storm, and the one following that, the sailor with a strong hand and steady voice responds to the Captains commands, "Hard to port, sailor".

"Hard to port she is, sir".

"Hard to starboard, sailor".

"Hard to starboard she is, sir".

The storms in life do not cease, but the sailor now has absolute faith and confidence in the Captain. They have come out of the darkness into the sunshine, from being blind to having clear vision, from doubt to certitude.

The sailor now prays for the storms with fervor, "Oh God send the storms, send me violent storms, so that I can show my Captain that I do truly love Him and my trust is absolute."

The storms, trials and tribulations, with or without the prayer, with or without the Captain continue. They will continue as long as he is upon this sea of life. Some of the tests he passes and some he fails, but those he fails he takes over and over again until with the loving help of the Captain he finally passes them.

Little by little, slowly by slowly, drop by drop the sailor becomes so in tune with the Captain that he sees with the Captain's eyes, hears with the Captain's ears and understands with the Captain's perceptions. His will is so merged with the Captain's that the sailor and Captain become one.

To explain these spiritual concepts in a physical world is indeed a formidable task and we can only use these physical and material things to try to understand a spiritual truth. In the same way Bahá'u'lláh uses such terms as songs, king, melody, throne and carpet etc., to try and convey a truth that is beyond words and beyond a physical existence.

> It is clear to thine Eminence that all the variations which the wayfarer in the stages of his journey beholdeth in the realms of being, proceed from his own vision. We shall give an example of this, that its meaning may become fully clear: Consider the visible sun; although it shineth with one radiance upon all things, and at the behest of the King of Manifestation bestoweth light on all creation, yet in each place it becometh manifest and shedeth its bounty according to the potentialities of that place. For instance, in a mirror it reflecteth its own disk and shape, and this is

due to the sensitivity of the mirror; in a crystal it maketh fire to appear, and in other things it showeth only the effect of its shining, but not its full disk. And yet, through that effect, by the command of the Creator, it traineth each thing according to the quality of that thing, as thou observest.

By training us each according to what we have been created for we can get the vision of the great value of every human being. The Manifestations of God are those clean, clear and spotless Mirrors of that invisible and unknowable Essence God. However, all men have been created to reflect according to their capacity and effort some part of this light.

Once upon a time there was a basket of jewels. The most beautiful diamonds, emeralds, rubies, sapphires and every other precious stone was contained in this basket. Also, in the center of the basket was a little black stone. The sun shone upon the basket and the colours of the rainbow were reflected from the diamonds, greens, blues, reds and every other colour, gleamed and danced, in the sun light. The basket was filled with bright and beautiful colours and light and fire seemed to mingle together.

The diamond said, "Look at me. Did you ever see such beautiful colours of the rainbow, as have been bestowed upon me? Why is that ugly little black stone in the middle of our beautiful basket?"

The emerald replied, "Yes, and look at me. Have you ever seen such a deep and glorious green as I possess. I hope someone will soon remove that black monstrosity from our midst".

The ruby with its deep and lustrous red, and every other stone in the basket, had some wonderful comment to make about themselves and something derogatory to say about the little black stone in the heart of the basket. Even the onyx spoke of its shining black and condemned to apparent worthlessness the little black stone.

Then in the evening the sun went down, all the light and fire were extinguished in the basket. The cold of the night descended and yet the basket was kept warm by the little black stone. All day while the jewels were glorying in their beauty, the little black stone was busy absorbing the sunshine and saving and storing it to keep the others warm through the long cold night. If only the jewels could have looked ahead to the worth of even the least of a loving creator's handiwork they would have one and all been appreciative of the little black stone.

Mankind, one and all, are like the jewels and black stones in this basket of life and the variations come from our own limited vision. If we can reach this valley of unity, all we will then see is our Creator reflected in His creation.

> *In like manner, colours become visible in every object according to the nature of that object. For instance, in a yellow globe, the rays shine yellow; in a white the rays are white; and in a red, the red rays are manifest. Then these variations are from the object, not from the shining light. And if a place be shut away from the light, as by walls or a roof, it will be entirely bereft of the splendour of the light, nor will the sun shine thereon.*

When we study the refraction of light, we shine the light through a prism and the light is broken down to its basic colours and, of course, we see the red, white, yellow, blue etc. When we bring these colours and focus them back together we get once again pure uncoloured light. When mankind becomes united it will focus attention on this oneness as reflected in these Manifestations of God, then all that will be seen is once again that pure light of God.

He also points out that if I cut myself off from the light it will be even as a wall and roof that will entirely shut out this spiritual light of my life.

> *Thus it is that certain invalid souls have confined the lands of knowledge within the wall of self and passion, and clouded them with ignorance and blindness, and have been veiled from the light of the mystic sun and the mysteries of the Eternal Beloved; they have strayed*

> after from the jeweled wisdom of the lucid Faith of the Lord of Messengers, have been shut out of the sanctuary of the All-Beauteous One, and banished from the Ka'bih of splendour. Such is the worth of the people of this age!

This tells us that these walls are the walls of self and passion and the roof is the roof of ignorance and blindness. Of course like the story of the sailor above when I kick my captain off my ship I lose my way. God does not shut me out but by my own choice I shut myself out. All we have to do is look at ourselves and our world today to realize that we have banished ourselves from the goal of the nearness to God.

> And if a nightingale soar upward from the clay off self and dwell in the rose bower of the heart, and in Arabian melodies and sweet Iranian songs recount the mysteries of God—a single word of which quickeneth to fresh, new life the bodies of the dead, and bestoweth the Holy Spirit upon the moldering bones of this existence—thou wilt behold a thousand claws of envy, a myriad beaks of rancor hunting after Him and with all their power intent upon His death.

This heavenly bird, the nightingale, could refer to you and I. It is not capitalized so it doesn't refer to the Manifestation. Bahá'u'lláh wrote in Arabic and in the Iranian languages and if we recount His story and His message of love and unity to give a new spiritual life to mankind. People filled with envy, hate and jealousy, will arise and with all their power try to silence us. This was the cause of Bahá'u'lláh's imprisonments, banishments, beatings and even His poisoning. This also was the cause of the crucifixion of Christ.

> Yea, to the beetle a sweet fragrance seemeth foul, and to the man sick of a rheum a pleasant perfume is as naught. Wherefore, it hath been said for the guidance of the ignorant:
>
> Cleanse thou the rheum from out thine head
> And breathe the breath of God instead.

A rheum is a head cold that plugs up one's nose. So we must clean out our spiritual nose in order to inhale the divine fragrance of God.

In sum, the differences in objects have now been made plain. Thus when the wayfarer gazeth only upon the place of appearance—that is, when he seeth only the many-colored globes—he beholdeth yellow and red and white; hence it is that conflict hath prevailed among the creatures, and a darksome dust from limited souls hath hid the world. And some do gaze upon the effulgence of the light; and some have drunk of the wine of oneness and these see nothing but the sun itself.

For a better understanding of this paragraph we can go back to where the mention was made about the Manifestations being the light bulbs of our day. The conflict is that some see the red bulb of Christ and others the white bulb of Buddha. Now if we are in this valley of unity we will be lovers of the light and we will not contend about the colour of the globes.

Thus, for that they move on these three differing planes, the understanding and the words of the wayfarers have differed; and hence the sign of conflict doth continually appear on earth. For some there are who dwell upon the plane of oneness and speak of that world, and some inhabit the realms of limitation, and some the grades of self, while others are completely veiled. Thus do the ignorant people of the day, who have no portion of the radiance of Divine Beauty, make certain claims, and in every age and cycle inflict on the people of the sea of oneness what they themselves deserve. "Should God punish men for their perverse doings, He would not leave on earth a moving thing! But to an appointed term doth He respite them...."

The idea of God punishing men for what they do and giving them a respite is very important. Respite means that

The Seven Valleys of Bahá'u'lláh

it is put off for a time but will eventually take place. Bahá'u'lláh also explains that this punishment is self-inflicted when it comes. A good example is the story in the Bible about Sodom and Gomorrah.

Abraham sat at the door to his tent. The midday sun caused the heat waves to dance and shimmer across the plain. Suddenly he saw three men coming. They seemed to float toward him and the intense sun made them seem to be made a light. Abraham jumped up from in front of his tent and rushed forward to meet the strangers. He bowed to the ground and invited them to honour his home by staying there. The three strangers agreed and as Abraham was a good host he had a feast prepared for his guests.

The heat of the day slowly gave way to the cool of the evening and Abraham and his guests relaxed after a good meal. He asked the strangers where they were going and what was their mission.

"We have been commissioned by God to go to those wicked cities of Sodom, Gomorrah, Admah and Zeboim and destroy them completely", was their reply.

Abraham's brother Lot and his family were living in Sodom and Abraham was afraid for his brother. He tried to convince these Angels to spare the city. But these cities were filled with drunkenness, lechery, fornications, homosexuals, lesbians, wild dancing and all manner of promiscuity. Not to mention the cheating, stealing and all types of crime. They were veritable centers of trade and commerce and the worship of gold had transplanted the worship of God. The conclusion was that they were to be annihilated. So Abraham directed them to his brother's house in Sodom.

When these Angels came to the house of Lot they were received with the same honour and respect that they had been accorded by Abraham. Some of the people of Sodom had seen these beautiful, handsome men go into Lot's house. Soon a large crowd gathered in front of the house and were demanding that Lot turn over these strangers that they could vent their sick and obscene vices on them. Of course Lot refused and even offered his own daughters in order to protect the strangers. The crowd was becoming angry and were pressing toward the door of Lot's house intent on killing Lot and taking the strangers by force. The Angels pulled Lot back into the house locked and bolted the door and the mob were suddenly struck momentarily blind.

The Angels then commanded Lot to take his family and flee the city at once. Lot pleaded with his sons-in-law to come with him. They refused: after all they had their businesses, their pigs and chickens and occupations so that it was not possible to go. The Angels further told Lot and his wife and daughters that they were not even to look back. If their hearts carried the least desire for any part of the wickedness of these cities and they were to look back even for a second they would turn into a pillars of salt.

Lot, obedient to the angels, fled toward the mountain. His wife felt the pangs of loss at leaving their home and everything of the world that she possessed and she did look back and was instantly turned into a pillar of salt.

The next day from the safety of the mountain Lot looked out upon the plain where these cities had been and he saw a dense cloud even the grass and vegetation was completely gone. Not a living thing was left upon this plain of waywardness and disobedience.

Our world today with its total loss of moral values and pursuits of pleasures is certainly a description of Sodom and Gomorrah. As stated in The Seven Valleys, in the Valley of Unity Bahá'u'lláh clearly states that we are living in a time of respite and I can't help but feel that this respite is about to run out.

> *O My Brother! A pure heart is as a mirror; cleanse it with the burnish of love and severance from all save God, that the true sun may shine within it and the eternal morning dawn. Then wilt thou clearly see the meaning of "Neither doth My earth nor My heaven contain Me, but the heart of My faithful servant containeth Me". And thou wilt take up thy life in*

The Seven Valleys of Bahá'u'lláh

thine hand, and with infinite longing cast it before the new Beloved One.

Over and over again Bahá'u'lláh is asking us to purify our heart and here he tells us that what is needed to make our hearts pure is love and severance. Severance means detachment and as Bahá'u'lláh tells us that the good things of the earth were put here for mankind's pleasure and enjoyment, what does detachment then mean? It is not what we have, but our attachment to these things. When I was in India one of the gurus (a spiritual teacher) explained to me the meaning of Bahá'í detachment.

India is a land of over 900 million people and the majority or whom live in the most abject poverty. What could detachment have to do with these people and what do they have to be detached from? One of the men who had been a guru said, "Let me explain the true meaning of detachment with this example". He then related the following story:

"Now in India we have an order of the detached ones and they are called Sadus. The Sadus takes a holly vow of detachment and his goal is to reach Nirvana or heaven. The Sadu, because he is detached from the world, has as his only possessions a begging bowl and a loin cloth. He is thought by the working population to be nearer to God. So an ordinary working man who is trying to make ends meet and is working from dawn to dusk just to keep body and soul together has no time for spiritual pursuits. The solution is to give money or food to the Sadus in his begging bowl. The Sadus who is very near to God prays for you and supplicates heaven on your behalf. This, of course, is even better than praying for yourself because you realize that you are very far from God and you can just get on with trying to make a living."

"Once upon a time there were two friends who together joined the order of Sadus. They traveled and studied at the feet of a famous Sadu guru. They became his disciples and for many years they were inseparable companions. One day their teacher called them to him, told them he could teach them no more and they must now go out on the highway of life and find their way, God willing, to the hidden path to Nirvana. He explained that the first step in total detachment was for them to even detach themselves from their friendship."

"Many years passed, youth gave way to maturity, and maturity finally yielded to old age. One day one of the Sadus heard of a very famous holy man who lived in the neighborhood and he determined to visit him. He arrived at the gate of a veritable palace. Servants were everywhere, fountains, gardens, lawns, swimming pools and even a Rolls Royce car in the driveway. He rang the door bell and when a servant arrived the Sadus asked if he might see and talk to the holy man. The little beggar was taken into the palace and was soon in the presence of the holy one. What magnificence! His clothes were of silk, his shirt had rubies for buttons, a diamond shone and glittered from the center of his turban and on his feet were the finest hand tooled cowboy boots from Texas. The little beggar wondered to himself 'how could such a prince with so many possessions be a true holy man.'"

"The holy man suddenly jumped up rushed up to the beggar took him into his arms and kissed him. Tears ran down his face as he explained that he was the beggar's companion of their youth. The little beggar was enraged, 'what of your vows of detachment? What of the search for Nirvana. How could you do such a thing?"

"The holy man said, 'God have mercy upon me, but I enjoy the gifts and bounties God has seen fit to bestow upon me. Now tell me old friend how goes your search for Nirvana."

"The little beggar answered, 'I am going right from your house directly to Nirvana. I have found the hidden path, the secret way."

"The holy man's eyes turned bright and he implored, "Please, take me with you, Oh! please, take me with you."

"The little beggar responded with a smile, 'Of course, old friend come along.'"

"The holy man tore off his turban, stripped off his clothes down to his loin cloth and the two friends together walked out of the palace and out of the compound. The holy man never looked right or left, he never looked back, but with shining face went forward. About a kilometer from the palace the little beggar stopped and said, 'Please, we must go back, we can not go to Nirvana yet.''

"'Don't hesitate, man if you know the way let's get on with it.' responded the holy man.

"'I can't, I can't, cried the beggar, 'I left my begging bowl at your house.'"

So the guru ended his narrative, with the observation, "Which of these two were really detached?"

Here in this Valley of Unity we learn a most valuable lesson, and that is in one's own heart is the place where we can find God. Not on the mountain top, not in nature and not even in the churches, temples and shrines of the world. We will find God in the love of His Manifestation enthroned in our own hearts, and nowhere else. The Captain is aboard our ship of physical existence. When this happens we are ready to sacrifice even our lives in the pathway of God.

> *Whensoever the light of Manifestation of the King of Oneness settleth upon the throne of the heart and soul, His shining becometh visible in every limb and member. At that time the mystery of the famed tradition gleameth out of the darkness: "A servant is drawn unto Me in prayer until I answer him; and when I have answered him, I become the ear wherewith he heareth...." For thus the Master of the house hath appeared within His home, and all the pillars of the dwelling are ashine with His light. And the action and effect of the light are from the Light-Giver; so it is that all move through Him and arise by His will. And this is that spring whereof the near ones drink, as it is said: "A fount whereof the near unto God shall drink...."*

An example of this is like a vacant and empty house. It is cold and gives one a feeling of desolation. Then the owner comes home, the fire is lit, the lights are turned on and the whole house changes into an inviting place of warmth, light, joy and happiness. So when the light of the Manifestation of God enters and dwells in one's heart that person develops the same characteristics as the house does when the owner enters his home.

> *However, let none construe these utterances to be anthropomorphism, nor see in them the descent of the worlds of God into the grades of the creatures; nor should they lead thine eminence to such assumptions. For God is, in His Essence, holy above ascent and descent, entrance and exit; He hath through all eternity been free of the attributes of human creatures, and ever will remain so. No man hath ever known Him; no soul hath ever found the pathway to His Being. Every mystic knower hath wandered far astray in the valley of the knowledge of Him; every saint hath lost his way in seeking to comprehend His Essence. Sanctified is He above the understanding of the wise; exalted is He above the knowledge of the knowing! The way is barred and to seek it is impiety; His proof is His signs; His being is His evidence.*

Anthropomorphism is the belief that God exists in everything. God exists in rock, a plant, an animal, a man. This is like saying an artist is part of his picture. It is true we can see the style and the beauty of the mind of the artist in his picture. The artist, however never crawls into his picture to live. So it is with God. He is far and away above and beyond His creation. Creation and all that is has come into existence from His will and by his hand. Here God informs us that the way is closed. In other places He calls the Manifestation the tree beyond which there is no passing.

Think about this unknowable source of power and might. The Force that puts worlds and suns and infinity into motion. If we were to come into contact with this power it would be like a speck of dust approaching the sun. Even if our whole world was to fall into the sun it would not even fizzle as it would be consumed long before it reached the sun. This is true of the Unknowable Essence of God to an even a greater extent, for He is the creator of these infinite suns. Although God through His Messengers shows us a reflection of Himself, this reflection is in accordance with our capacity and ability, it is not even close to His Infinite Reality. The Teachers He sends with Their wisdom, knowledge and spirit, although far above our ability to know and understand, are still just a higher order of God's creation.

> *Wherefore, the lovers of the face of the Beloved have said: "O Thou, the One Whose Essence alone showeth the way to His Essence, and Who is sanctified above any likeness to His creatures." How can utter nothingness gallop its steed in the field of preexistence, or a fleeting shadow reach to the everlasting sun? The Friend hath said, "But for Thee, we had not known Thee," and the Beloved hath said, "nor attained Thy presence".*

It is the Manifestation of God, Bahá'u'lláh, that is the Essence that shows us the way to God's Essence. Bahá'u'lláh is the Friend and He is the Beloved and to attain the presence of Bahá'u'lláh and/or any of the other Manifestations of Holiness is to come as near to our Creator God as we can ever hope to get. When He explains about settling in the heart of man and finding God in our own hearts, this is, and can only be, in the station of the Manifestation.

> *Yea, these mentionings that have been made of the grades of knowledge relate to the knowledge of the Manifestations of that Sun of Reality, which casteth Its light upon the Mirrors. And the splendor of that light is in the hearts, yet it is hidden under the veilings of sense and the conditions of this earth, even as a*

candle within a lantern of iron, and only when the lantern is removed doth the light of the candle shine out.

God has created us and He created this light within us and it is these great Teachers of God that turn on the switch. However, we must clear our hearts of the debris of our sense and conditions of this material existence. Then the light of God will shine out from us. A candle is a good example, for it weeps its life away drop by drop in order to give forth light to others.

In like manner, when thou strippest the wrappings of illusion from off thine heart, the lights of oneness will be made manifest.

An illusion is something that seems to be real but isn't. Our great magicians are masters of illusion. Here we must look for reality and not be taken in by illusion.

Then it is clear that even for the rays there is neither entrance nor exit—how much less for that Essence of Being and that longed-for Mystery. O My Brother, journey upon these planes in the spirit of search, not in blind imitation. A true wayfarer will not be kept back by the bludgeon of words nor debarred by the warning of allusions.

How shall a curtain part the lover and the loved one? Not Alexander's wall can separate them!

This is true for the light was created within us when we were created. The concept of a bludgeon is a club of great size used to beat people to death. The whole world is sick and tired of words, words and more words. We all want to see action. Please don't tell me anymore, just show me.

It is a well known fact that true lovers will always find a way to get together. So it should be with us and our Divine Teachers.

Secrets are many, but strangers are myriad. Volumes will not suffice to hold the mystery of the Beloved

> One, nor can it be exhausted in these pages, although it be no more than a word, no more than a sign. "Knowledge is a single point, but the ignorant have multiplied it".

Although the secrets of God have been revealed to us in over one hundred books, Tablets and the revelation from Bahá'u'lláh, strangers to these truths are beyond counting. Myriad means a number that can't be counted. For example, the grass is myriad in the field. We know there is a certain number of blades of grass in the field but no one can count them.

Although knowledge is only a single letter, because of our ignorance we multiply that knowledge. This is exactly what I am doing with these seven valleys. I prove my ignorance by trying to explain something that is far beyond my ability and capacity, which is the word of God.

> On this same basis, ponder likewise the differences among the worlds. Although the divine worlds be never ending, yet some refer to them as four: The world of time (zaman), which is the one that hath both a beginning and an end; the world of duration (dahr), which hath a beginning, but whose end is not revealed; the world of perpetuity (sarmad), whose beginning is not to be seen but which is known to have an end; and the world of eternity (azal), neither a beginning nor an end of which is visible. Although there are many differing statements as to these points, to recount them in detail would result in weariness. Thus, some have said that the world of perpetuity hath neither beginning nor end, and have named the world of eternity as the invisible, impregnable Empyrean. Others have called these the worlds of the Heavenly Court (Láhút), of the Empyrean Heaven (Jabarút), of the Kingdom of the Angels (Malakút), and of the mortal world (Násút).

Here Bahá'u'lláh tells us that the divine worlds are unending. He seems to be making the point of how knowledge is a single point and the ignorant multiply it. He tells us that some divide the world into four parts, time, duration, perpetuity and eternity. Others disagree with this and divide it up in other ways. This is clear from His statement that "some refer to them" and "others have called these".

> The journeys in the pathway of love are reckoned as four: From the creatures to the True One; from the True One to the creatures; from the creatures to the creatures; from the True One to the True One.

This means the love of man for God, the love of God for man, the love of man for his fellow men and the love of God for Himself as reflected in His Manifestation.

> There is many an utterance of the mystic seers and doctors of former times which I have not mentioned here, since I mislike the copious citation from sayings of the past; for quotation from the words of others proveth acquired learning, not the divine bestowal. Even so much as We have quoted here is out of deference to the wont of men and after the manner of the friends. Further, such matters are beyond the scope of this epistle. Our unwillingness to recount their sayings is not from pride, rather is it a manifestation of wisdom and a demonstration of grace:
>
> If Khidr did wreck the vessel on the sea,
> Yet in this wrong there are a thousand rights.
>
> Otherwise, this Servant regardeth Himself as utterly lost and as nothing, even beside one of the beloved of God, how much less in the presence of His holy ones. Exalted be My Lord, the Supreme! Moreover, our aim is to recount the stages of the wayfarer's journey, not to set forth the conflicting utterances of the mystics.

Bahá'u'lláh's knowledge came as a direct revelation from God. He also, in this passage shows mankind His extreme humility. He points out that these so-called holy men and mystics are in continual conflict with each other and their teachings.

> Although a brief example hath been given concerning the beginning and ending of the relative world, the world of attributes, yet a second illustration is now added, that the full meaning may be manifest. For instance, let thine Eminence consider his own self; thou art first in relation to thy son, last in relation to thy father. In thine outward appearance, thou tellest of the appearance of power in the realms of divine creation; in thine inward being thou revealest the hidden mysteries which are the divine trust deposited within thee. And thus firstness and lastness, outwardness and inwardness are, in the sense referred to, true of thyself, that in these four states conferred upon thee thou shouldst comprehend the four divine states, and that the nightingale of thine heart on all the branches of the rose tree of existence, whether visible or concealed, should cry out: "He is the first and the last, the Seen and the Hidden...."

Man has been created in the image of God so in this passage Bahá'u'lláh is teaching us that the qualities of the Manifestation of God can also be found in man. In a being like Bahá'u'lláh they are complete and perfected to a degree that we can't understand or attain to.

These Manifestations of God are the first and the last, the Seen and the Hidden. They are first in relation to mankind, last in relation to God. In their outward appearance they manifest the Power and Might of God. In Their inner being lies hidden the mysteries of Divine Trust that God has created them for.

> These statements are made in the sphere of that which is relative, because of the limitations of men. Otherwise, those personages who in a single step have passed over the world of the relative and the limited, and dwelt on the fair plane of the Absolute, and pitched their tent in the worlds of authority and

command—have burned away these relativities with a single spark, and blotted out these words with a drop of dew. And they swim in the sea of the spirit, and soar in the holy air of light. Then what life have words, on such a plane, that "first" and "last" or other than these be seen or mentioned! In this realm, the first is the last itself, and the last is but the first.

> In thy soul of love build thou a fire
> And burn all thoughts and words entire.

Bahá'u'lláh now brings us back to the valley of unity which is the state beyond words, names and attributes. He explains that He makes these statements because men live in those three previous valleys which are the valleys of limitations. Those also that are not even in the valleys need more explanation. If one is truly in the valley of unity all that can be seen is oneness.

> O my friend, look upon thyself: Hadst thou not become a father nor begotten a son, neither wouldst thou have heard these sayings. Now forget them all, that thou mayest learn from the Master of Love in the schoolhouse of oneness, and return unto God, and forsake the inner land of unreality for thy true station, and dwell within the shadow of the tree of knowledge.

True knowledge can only be learned from the Divine Master and Bahá'u'lláh is inviting us to our own true destines in life.

> O thou dear one! Impoverish thyself, that thou mayest enter the high court of riches; and humble thy body, that thou mayest drink from the river of glory, and attain to the full meaning of the poems where of thou hadst asked.

The path to true riches and true glory is given here in this passage. The ocean has been placed at the lowest level and as such all the waters of the earth flow into it. We must also understand that to impoverish oneself is to not be attached to anyone or anything. Bahá'u'lláh even goes so far as to elevate our work to a station of worship and to forbid begging. He commands us to earn our living and to take care of our responsibilities. This is like the sailor on the ship discarding all the garbage of his life and straightening out the tangled lines of his life.

> Thus it hath been made clear that these stages depend on the vision of the wayfarer. In every city he will behold a world, in every Valley reach a spring, in every meadow hear a song. But the falcon of the mystic heaven hath many a wondrous carol of the spirit in His breast, and the Persian bird keepeth in His soul many a sweet Arab melody; yet these are hidden, and hidden shall remain.
>
> > If I speak forth, many a mind will shatter,
> > And if I write, many a pen will break.
>
> Peace be upon him who concludeth this exalted journey and followeth the True One by the lights of guidance.

As Christ said, "I have many things to tell you but you can not bear them now. Howbeit when He, the Spirit of truth, is come, He will guide you unto all truth". When Bahá'u'lláh came He declared that He was the One promised by Christ. He revealed numerous Books and Tablets. Yet here in The Seven Valleys Bahá'u'lláh tells us that there is still an abundance of truth that He has that can't be given to mankind.

> And the wayfarer, after traversing the high planes of this supernal journey, entereth

THE VALLEY OF CONTENTMENT

> In this Valley he feeleth the winds of divine contentment blowing from the plane of the spirit. He burneth away the veils of want, and with inward and

> *outward eye, perceiveth within and without all things the day of: "God will compensate each one out of His abundance". From sorrow he turneth to bliss, from anguish to joy. His grief and mourning yield to delight and rapture.*

Our wayfarer, if he can reach this sublime station, wants for nothing. In this valley the inward eye of the spirit or the eye of man's soul is wide open and sees all. The gifts that descend from God in this station are endless. No longer will this wayfarer be sorrowful, anguished or grieved. One in the Valley of Contentment is a happy and joyful being.

> *Although to outward view, the wayfarers in this Valley may dwell upon the dust, yet inwardly they are throned in the heights of mystic meaning; they eat of the endless bounties of inner significance, and drink of the delicate wines of the spirit.*

This makes it clear that this valley of contentment can be attained while still living in this physical world. Although we live in this world of dust the souls of the people who dwell in the Valley of Contentment soar into the highest heaven. The heart of man is the wellspring of divine treasure, here these gems are mined, polished and revealed through the help of the Divine Teacher.

> *The tongue faileth in describing these three Valleys, and speech falleth short. The pen steppeth not into this region, the ink leaveth only a blot. In these planes, the nightingale of the heart hath other songs and secrets, which make the heart to stir and the soul to clamor, but this mystery of inner meaning may be whispered only from heart to heart, confided only from breast to breast.*

> *Only heart to heart can speak the bliss of mystic knowers;*
> *No messenger can tell it and no missive bear it.*

> *I am silent from weakness on many a matter,*
> *For my words could not reckon them and my speech would fall short.*

True feelings and emotions are impossible to describe. For example, try to describe love. Whatever your words are they will fall short of describing the feelings of love that surge within the human heart. So it is with the other spiritual attributes and true spiritual experiences. If two people have the same or like experiences then words are not needed to convey these feelings. So it evidently is the same in The Valley of Contentment.

> *O friend, till thou enter the garden of such mysteries, thou shalt never set lip to the undying wine of this Valley. And shouldst thou taste of it, thou wilt shield thine eyes from all things else, and drink of the wine of contentment; and thou wilt loose thyself from all things else, and bind thyself to Him, and throw thy life down in His path, and cast thy soul away. However, there is no other in this region that thou need forget: "There was God and there was naught beside Him". For on this plane the traveler witnesseth the beauty of the Friend in everything. Even in fire, he seeth the face of the Beloved. He beholdeth in illusion the secret of reality, and readeth from the attributes the riddle of the Essence. For he hath burnt away the veils with his sighing, and unwrapped the shroudings with a single glance; with piercing sight he gazeth on the new creation; with lucid heart he graspeth subtle verities. This is sufficiently attested by: "And we have made thy sight sharp in this day".*

With that inner vision of the eyes of the soul this traveler sees God made manifest throughout creation. Because one now can see God reflected in all things and all conditions, such a one is ready to sacrifice his all in this path. This vision is a new creation, although it was potentially in the being of man, it is like the fruit is also potentially in the fruit tree. Now it springs forth in an abundant harvest from the mine of man's heart.

After journeying through the planes of pure contentment, the traveler cometh to

THE VALLEY OF WONDERMENT

and is tossed in the oceans of grandeur, and at every moment his wonder growth. Now he seeth the shape of wealth as poverty itself, and the essence of freedom as sheer impotence. Now is he struck dumb with the beauty of the All-Glorious; again is he wearied out with his own life. How many a mystic tree hath this whirlwind of wonderment snatched by the roots, how many a soul hath it exhausted. For in this Valley the traveler is flung into confusion, albeit, in the eye of him who hath attained,, such marvels are esteemed and well beloved. At every moment he beholdeth a wondrous world, a new creation, and goeth from astonishment to astonishment, and is lost in awe at the works of the Lord of Oneness.

The Valley of Contentment is not just contentment but is one of pure contentment. Like having a pure heart, pure contentment is not contaminated with anything.

From contentment the wayfarer goes into the valley of wonderment. It seems that this valley is a step up from contentment. Bahá'u'lláh uses the words confusion, wearied, exhausted and snatched by the roots in trying to describe this valley to us. These happenings seem to be because our traveler is overwhelmed by the nearness and greatness of God being manifested to him through all things. The wayfarer sees at every moment new worlds and new creations being formed before his very own spiritual eyes and in witnessing such things goes from astonishment to astonishment.

Indeed, O Brother, if we ponder each created thing, we shall witness a myriad perfect wisdoms and learn a

> myriad new and wondrous truths. One of the created phenomena is the dream. Behold how many secrets are deposited therein, how many wisdoms treasured up, how many worlds concealed. Observe, how thou art asleep in a dwelling, and its doors are barred; on a sudden thou findest thyself in a far-off city, which thou enterest without moving thy feet or wearying thy body; without using thine eyes, thou seest; without taxing thine ears, thou hearest; without a tongue, thou speakest. And perchance when ten years are gone, thou wilt witness in the outer world the very things thou hast dreamed tonight.

Remember that this word myriad means too many to count, and as we meditate on God's creation from the smallest to the largest, we will discover a myriad truths in each and every one of them.

Bahá'u'lláh then goes on to describe the dream and I have had this happen to me many times in my own life. That is I may dream something to day and have it come to pass exactly as I saw it in my dream some years later.

About 1952 I had one of those deep spiritual experiences that have affected my entire life. Word had been received in the American Bahá'í community that the door was once again open for the pilgrims to visit the World Center in Haifa, Israel. The pilgrimages had been stopped because of the second world war. Shoghi Effendi, the great grandson of Bahá'u'lláh, and the leader of the world Bahá'í community, was extending an invitation. Upon receipt of this information, my soul was seized with such longing as is indescribable. However, I was still attached to my material civilization, I assumed that it was financially impossible to accept such an invitation. Oh, if I had only had the detachment I now possess, I would have been privileged to have met and known Shoghi Effendi, but I denied myself this privilege. The average American goes into debt for house, car, appliances, vacations and everything else but for the most precious and wholly spiritual gift of all. He cannot afford it! My heart and soul said, "Go, even of you must walk", but my mind and satanic fancy argued, "No, don't go, for you cannot afford to". In those early days my mind ruled my heart, but such was my inner agitation and longing that I soon could think of nothing else but Haifa, Báhji, Acca and Shoghi Effendi. My work began to suffer, my nights were sleepless, and I even lost my appetite—and so I wasted away in my valley of inner longing.

However, my deliverance was at hand and took place in the following manner: We had hosted an especially beautiful meeting in our home and the friends had left. My wife and children were asleep. As I sat up, reading once again this very Book The Seven Valleys, I soon became so enamored and immersed in that heavenly Book that for the first time in many days, my agitation of heart was stilled, and a tranquility pervaded my soul, the like of which I had never known. The very air became charged with peace and nearness to God. Finally, having quenched my thirst at the fountain of life, I put down the Book and retired to bed. No sooner had my head hit the pillow than I was in the Holy Land. I fully realized that my body was in Great Falls, Montana lying upon its bed but my spirit, flying free, had accomplished what the body refused to do.

The room which I was in appeared to be of concrete, with a window on my left and another window straight ahead. The window on my left had a very low, wide ledge and upon this ledge was lying the Blessed Beauty, Bahá'u'lláh. How I prayed, but still he lay with his back to me. Then I went out of the room to tell Shoghi Effendi (Great Grandson of Bahá'u'lláh) that Bahá'u'lláh had His back to me. He said, "You go right back in there and pray for someone other than yourself".

This time Bahá'u'lláh was facing me and the reality of prayer set aflame my entire being as I prayed for others, with complete abandon. That beautiful face was beyond description, but most extraordinary were the eyes. Now, for the first time in my life I knew adoration, devotion and selflessness. As my prayer raced heavenward, such heavenly singing was heard surrounding me that the roof of that room opened up and I felt myself ascending. As I stated, I realized my body was upon the bed in Great Falls, but it seemed to me that not only my spirit but my body also was rising. Upon this realization, the vision ended and I came back so abruptly that I shook the bed and awakened my wife. I closed my eyes and cried out, "Oh Bahá'u'lláh, please come back and I vow that my body and self will not be allowed to interfere". But the vision ended, and I fell into a deep and dreamless sleep.

Having made this spiritual pilgrimage, my heart was at rest, my soul content. I fully realize that such spiritual experiences are not unusual among the friends and I also know that the meaning of these experiences is for the heart of the recipient, but I have recorded this incident here because in my life it has been a guiding light and will always remain a confirmation for me of the nearness of God.

It was in 1964 when I was able to make my pilgrimage to Haifa. Shoghi Effendi had passed away in 1957 so I missed the opportunity to see him. When we visited the prison city of Akká and the cell where Bahá'u'lláh had been confined, I was completely unprepared for what happened at the Prison. At the cell of Bahá'u'lláh I removed my shoes. The door was opened and I stepped into the cell. The impact was more than I could stand and my heart shattered into a thousand bits. To begin with, the cell, in every detail, was the room of my vision of twelve years past, when I had seen Bahá'u'lláh face to face.

> *Now there are many wisdoms to ponder in the dream, which none but the people of this Valley can comprehend in their true elements. First, what is this world, where without eye and ear and hand and tongue a man puts all of these to use? Second, how is it that in the outer world thou seest today the effect of a dream, when thou didst vision it in the world of sleep some ten years past? Consider the difference*

> between these two worlds and the mysteries which they conceal, that thou mayest attain to divine confirmations and heavenly discoveries and enter the regions of holiness.

As Bahá'u'lláh stated there are many divine wisdoms in our dreams and this seems to indicate the oneness of God's creation by showing us that in some way all the worlds of creation are inter-relateed. We explored this oneness a little in the Valley of Unity, but here in this valley it takes us to a higher step of unity by including the hidden and invisible worlds of God.

The story related earlier about Joseph also can explain something of what Bahá'u'lláh is trying to teach us in the valley of wonderment. The dreams that are related in those stories actually happened just as Joseph said they would. The story related above of my own experiences also is a spiritual confirmation for me of the dream. In another Tablet of Bahá'u'lláh, He explains that the dream is also another proof of the existence of the human soul and of life after death because in the world of dreams we move, speak hear and see without those organs that make these actions possible.

> God, the Exalted, hath placed these signs in men, to the end that philosophers may not deny the mysteries of the life beyond nor belittle that which hath been promised them. For some hold to reason and deny whatever the reason comprehendeth not, and yet weak minds can never grasp the matters which we have related, but only the Supreme, Divine Intelligence can comprehend them:
>
> How can feeble reason encompass the Qur'án,
> Or the spider snare a phoenix in his web?

Bahá'u'lláh clearly teaches us that there is life beyond death and further that we will have to answer at that time for our actions or inactions in life. The religious Books of the past are filled with the promise of God and the threat of punishment. I would like to again point out that this punishment is self-inflicted.

A very tender and loving father was watching his only baby son play and the baby started to touch the fire. "No! No! My little son", shouted the father and he quickly moved the child away from the fire. But like all little children (and many adults) when told not to do something, that is exactly what they want to do and insist on doing. Soon the child was back at the fire and again the daddy stops the child even slapping the little one's hand trying to establish hurt and pain in the tot's mind. However, soon the baby succeeds with its will and when daddy is not looking burns its fingers. Did this loving father put the hand into the fire? No, of course not, and our loving Creator who loves us to a degree beyond human understanding and far more than any parent can love his child, tells us, "Don't touch, you will burn your fingers". We disobey, we burn our fingers.

Bahá'u'lláh teaches us here that the true inner meanings can only be understood by God's Teachers and He confirms this with the verse asking, "How can a human understand God's Holy Qur'án or how can a spider catch a phoenix in its web?" He explains that both ideas are absurdities.

> *All these states are to be witnessed in the Valley of Wonderment, and the traveler at every moment seeketh for more, and is not wearied. Thus the Lord of the First and the Last in setting forth the grades of contemplation, and expressing wonderment hath said: "O Lord, increase my astonishment at Thee!"*

Even the Manifestation of God is saying in this valley "O Lord, increase my astonishment at Thee!" If our minds and spirits are incapable of understanding and only the Teacher has been created with this understanding it will be through His grace and bounty that He will breathe into our souls an infinitesimal glimmer of its truth. Not through words will this be done. Only as He said, from Heart to heart and Mind to mind.

> Likewise, reflect upon the perfection of man's creation, and that all these planes and states are folded up and hidden away within him.
>
> > Dost thou recon thyself only a puny form
> > When within thee the universe is folded?
>
> Then we must labor to destroy the animal condition, till the meaning of humanity shall come to light.

This is an amazing statement, that all these planes are potentially within our proper selves. Like the fruit tree, we must grow in fertile soil, have adequate water and grow in the sunshine. The soil is the Teachings of God. We must go deep into this rich soil to draw up the life giving qualities. Then we must water it with prayer and put it into the radiant sunshine of obedience. It is certain that if we follow this formula the tree of our souls will grow, blossom and bear luscious fruit in its season.

It is through our obedience to the heaven sent Teachings that this animal nature of man will be destroyed and the true human being will come into existence. Hard work on our part is needed if we are to succeed.

Another truly amazing assurance is given to us in the teaching that the universe is folded up within us.

> Thus, too, Luqmán, who had drunk from the wellspring of wisdom and tasted of the waters of mercy, in proving to his son Nathan the planes of resurrection and death, advanced the dream as an evidence and an example. We relate it here, that through this evanescent Servant a memory may endure of that youth of the school of Divine Unity, that elder of the art of instruction and the Absolute. He said: "O Son, if thou art able not to sleep, then thou art able not to die. And if thou art able not to waken after sleep, then thou shalt be able not to rise after death."

In this passage Bahá'u'lláh again confirms the life of the soul after physical death.

> O friend, the heart is the dwelling of eternal mysteries, make it not the home of fleeting fancies; waste not the treasure of thy precious life in employment with this swiftly passing world. Thou comest from the world of holiness—bind not thine heart to the earth; thou art a dweller in the court of nearness—choose not the homeland of the dust.

We are born, we live, we die and our preoccupation with this world for that short span of years does not benefit us in anyway. The heart was created to be the dwelling place of the love of God and not for this material existence. We come from a world of holiness and like the drop returning to the ocean we shall certainly return to that world of holiness. Like the drop we must deposit the silt of self and worldly attachment on the delta of the river of life as it flows back into the sea. Still Bahá'u'lláh gives us a choice, for here he tells us to choose His court of nearness and not the empty homeland of dust, meaning the material existence.

> In sum, there is no end to the description of these stages, but because of the wrongs inflicted by the peoples of the earth, this Servant is in no mood to continue:
>
> The tale is still unfinished and I have no heart for it- Then pray forgive me.
> The pen groaneth and the ink sheddeth tears, and the river of the heart moveth in waves of blood. "Nothing can befall us but what God hath destined for us." Peace be upon him who followeth the Right Path!

Bahá'u'lláh mentions His extreme suffering here in this valley of wonderment. Remember He was beaten, chained, imprisoned, exiled, poisoned and slandered. Surely this is something to wonder at. We have the brilliant light of God shining radiantly in our midst and mankind as a whole disregards it entirely and some of the so called leaders of the earth try to extinguish His light. All the suffering of Bahá'u'lláh only caused His light to burn more brightly.

After scaling the high summits of wonderment the wayfarer cometh to

THE VALLEY OF TRUE POVERTY AND ABSOLUTE NOTHINGNESS

This station is the dying from self and the living in God, the being poor in self and rich in the Desired One. Poverty as here referred to signifieth being poor in the things of the created world, rich in the things of God's world. For when the true lover and devoted friend reacheth to the presence of the Beloved, the sparkling beauty of the Loved One and the fire of the lover's heart will kindle a blaze and burn away all veils and wrappings. Yea, all he hath, from heart to skin, will be set aflame, so that nothing will remain save the Friend.

When the qualities of the Ancient of Days stood revealed,
Then the qualities of earthly things did Moses burn away.

He who hath attained this station is sanctified from all that ertaineth to the world. Wherefore, if those who have come to the sea of His presence are found to possess none of the limited things of this perishable world, whether it be outer wealth or personal opinions, it mattereth not. For whatever the creatures have is limited by their own limits, and whatever the True One hath is sanctified therefrom; this utterance must be deeply pondered that its purport may be clear. "Verily the righteous shall drink of a winecup tempered at the camphor fountain". If the interpretation of "camphor" become known, the true intention will be evident. This state is that poverty of which it is said, "Poverty is My glory". And of inward and outward poverty there is many a stage and many a meaning which I have not thought pertinent to mention here; hence I have reserved these for another time, dependent on what God may desire and fate may seal.

The Valley of True Poverty and Absolute Nothingness seems to be where a person has completely sacrificed himself to God and nothing is left. No personal opinions, no veils, no wrappings, no outer wealth, no limits; even one's own thoughts are gone. The mystery of sacrifice is that there is no sacrifice. For example, the blossom is sacrificed for the fruit. The caterpillar is sacrificed for the butterfly. The worldly man is sacrificed into a heavenly being.

This drinking a cup tempered at the camphor fountain is mentioned in the Qur'án as well as by Bahá'u'lláh. From the other references it would seem to mean only those righteous souls who have dedicated and given their all to the cause of God can drink from this cup. Truly those servants who have attained to this station are of the highest order and have become angels.

Bahá'u'lláh also indicates here that there is an inner poverty as well as an outer poverty. I will use another analogy to try to understand this point.

At one time ever so long ago this swamp had been a clear clean and sweet flowing river. It is supposed to be the river of life. Now, however, its waters are stopped up by the debris from the jungle. The water has turned greer with algae, insects, lizards and snakes have made their homes in its putrid waters.

For the five to six thousand years of recorded history the human race, with few exceptions, has practiced willful disobedience to the loving instructions of a most loving Creator. Every divine teacher and all the world's great philosophers have told us that our Creator wants us to love each other. If history can be judged as a standard, we have ample proof that hating and warring doesn't work. For a very refreshing change why don't we give loving a break and give it an honest try. Of course, what would happen is the swamp would quickly drain away and the jungle would give way to flowered meadows and the sweet river of life would flow unimpeded to the sea of reunion and true happiness.

The Creator of the river of life and the Creator of the canoe and its occupant tell everyone to be loving. The command is almost universally ignored, instead mankind hates, murders and kills for its own greed and selfishness. Humanity, at least the majority, still worship the golden calf or the false god of materialism. People strive with heart and soul all the days of their lives for material gain and possessions only to leave them all behind at life's end. Over the generations of men the swamp is expanded and extended which in turn allows the jungle to creep in. Thus more and more of the river of life is converted to swamp and jungle.

The occupant (man's soul) of the canoe (man's body) lived in the swamp. He had paddled from one part of the swamp to another and pursued unrelentingly one small bit of jungle after the other. As he paddled, the jungle tore at him and his canoe. The sky was obscured by the thick tangled jungle. The snakes and insects were his constant companions and foes. He was ever alert for the marauding crocodiles and alligators which were intent upon his life, not to mention the other canoes trying by what ever devices they could to steal from him what little jungle he was able to obtain. When a small victory was achieved he soon realized that it was a hollow and empty victory, won at great expense to him and his canoe.

He watched helplessly as his mother and father, friends and relatives, even strangers, one and all, terminated their existence in the swamp sinking into oblivion in its putrid depths. He fully realized that one day he too, following in their footsteps, would surely and inevitably do likewise. What is the point? Why was he here? Where was he going? How come? These questions and many more weighed heavily on the occupant of the canoe, as he inexorably moved toward his sure fate.

One day, after another meaningless experience, he met another occupant. He spoke with much feeling about his doubts, anxieties and frustrations. This true friend listened then told the occupant about the river of life. He told him where it is flowing. Where one can see the blue sky and sense the clean air. A place free of all forms of pollution now prevalent in the swamp and jungle. He offered him a guide book, (The Seven Valleys of Bahá'u'lláh) which was gratefully accepted and diligently studied.

The occupant of the canoe said to himself, "Well, why not, I've tried everything else. I will probably be just chasing another dream, trying to find another pot of gold at the end of the rainbow. Yet, I must investigate on the off chance that it might be true. I'll have a go at it."

He studied carefully the guide Book, following the directions as best he could. He fought his way through the swamp. In the process he damaged many other canoes. He was torn, bitten by the snakes and insects, and bloodied by the jungle, but he didn't care. He just wanted out of the swamp and jungle. His motive was indeed very selfish. To the initiated this is base and unworthy, yet to the uninitiated it is the only way. "I want out, I want a purpose, I want to see the sky and breathe clean and sweet air". After all, all he had ever learned and known in the swamp and jungle was how to be selfish and greedy and think only of himself. He had been advised and taught by everyone, "You have to think only about number one. If you don't no one will".

With the aid of his guide Book which he diligently studied every day, he worked his way slowly out of the jungle and onto the river. He had made many a false turn, but by checking the guide book, he was able to learn from it and correct his mistakes. The jungle over his head slowly cleared away. He found the azure blue sky and from the constant gloom of the jungle he experienced the glorious sunshine. The stench of the jungle gave way to clean fresh air, scented with the flowers that lined the river bank. The stagnant water of the swamp yielded to the sweet fresh running water of the river. What joy pervaded his soul as he delighted in sight, sound, smell, taste and feel. This was a greater purpose and a truer happiness than anything he had ever experienced in the swamp.

His exquisite joy and happiness that he delighted in was doomed to be short-lived. As he paddled his canoe out into the currents of the river, he was so awed and overcome that he stopped paddling in order to fully enjoy the reality of the new life he had discovered. The currents of the river took control of the canoe and slowly and imperceptibly drew him back into the jungle and swamp. The occupant learned that all the currents of life are trying in every conceivable way to pull us back and keep us in the swamp. One has to put forth a great effort to fight the pull of the current. Only when one is willing to struggle against the current to go up river, can one attain the joys of the river of life.

Although the occupant was once more back deep into the swamp there was a difference, for now he had a vision. He knew there was more to life and living than the miserable jungle and foul swamp. He had tasted for a brief moment the exquisite sweetness of reality. With heartfelt determination he set his course for the river and this time he vowed that he would not let the currents pull him back or keep him back.

Once more he emerged into the river and it was even more beautiful than he had remembered. The currents pulled and tugged at his canoe and sometimes he did slip backwards a little yet he persevered, moving steadily and surely up the river. With every stroke of the paddle he experienced new delights. His paddling up the river of life towards God became almost automatic. His skill at navigating the river and anticipating the currents increased day by day. He became intoxicated with the wine of astonishment at the delights and beauties that he was exposed to. Although he was still in his canoe and still traversing the river of life he had found heaven on earth.

His unspoken prayers had been indeed answered. His life had purpose felt, and experienced through living. His goal was to ascend the river from self to God, to go from earth to heaven. Yes, he had even learned to battle the negative currents of the river with fortitude and determination. The feelings of security and safety began to pervade his soul. Surely he felt that powers and forces unheard of and unexplained had now come into play. His life had been given over to this Supreme Force with these thoughts and feelings a certain smugness and an idea crept into his subconsciousness that he was one of the chosen few.

His, "holier than thou", attitude was shattered into a thousand pieces as his canoe smashed into a boulder hidden in the rivers depths. He careened off the rock only to be rent by a snag in the river that tore open his canoe from stem to stern. Somehow he struggled to shore, managed to make repairs and proceeded on up the river.

With each mile he advanced beauty was compounded. The fragrant flowers lined the river bank. Sun beams danced in the mist of the river. Joy and happiness filled his heart and his soul delighted in each new discovery. This journey up the river did not take place without sustained and strenuous effort. Sometimes he would be caught in a whirlpool, spun around at incredible speed until he did not know which way was up river or which way was down river. Other times he hit the rocks or again and again was snagged and his canoe torn by deadwood that was concealed in the river's depths. His strength became monumental as he battled the unceasing currents and fought the perils that lie concealed in the river of life. He was also aware of unseen and undreamt of forces that came to assist him whenever he would become discouraged or feel he was unable to endure the struggle. He not only developed a great strength of body but he also developed this same great strength of soul.

No soul is tested beyond its capacity, for if it was it would be indicative of an unjust Creator. When the occupant was prepared by the river both physically and spiritually, he heard a strange roar up ahead. When he rounded the bend, he was faced with a barrier of white water thundering over the rapids. He moved his canoe into an eddy and carefully studied the situation. On both sides of the river there were cliffs going straight up. Making a portage around this seemingly insurmountable obstacle was out of the question. The river seemed to be saying to the occupant of the canoe, "Do you really believe? Do you really want to come up the river to Me? Can you really trust that unseen and undreamt of power that you have experienced in the lower heavens down river? Then come on up."

Some people when they reach this point in their journey give up and stop paddling. They let the currents that are ever ready pull them back into the hellish swamp. Our occupant considers his options. The full realization dawns upon him, his only true option is to face the rapids and make it up river or die in the attempt. He is not foolish or impulsive for the river has taught him much. He studies the rapids and with a deep felt prayer on his lips, "Oh God help me" he ploughs into the rapids. It requires all his skill, all of his inner and outer strength and all of the unseen but ever ready powers and forces that transcend human understanding to make it but make it he does. When he finally gets into the calm waters above the rapids he finds a heaven and delights far beyond anything he found down river. Words are meaningless and expressions inadequate to describe these upper reaches of the river.

The next time it is a waterfall, but with great difficulty the portage is made. The trip towards God is continued. Finally he reaches the head waters of the river and comes out onto a beautiful lake. The lake is surrounded by flowers and trees and gentle animals browse on the shore at the lake side. The current is still there, imperceptible, but ever present and ready to pull him back down the river and back into the jungle and swamp. However, the occupant is fully conscious of this and paddling his own canoe is second nature to him now.

He has indeed, with the help of heaven, reached the seventh heaven. Once he has discovered all the delights

The Seven Valleys of Bahá'u'lláh

and hidden secrets of this placeless place a new realization begins to manifest itself within him. Up to this point all his striving was selfish. "I want out, I want sweet water, I want beauty, I want delight and I want heaven for me." This step must be taken and it is the only way. This first step is selfish.

Now, however the next step is the complete abandonment of self. With all this wonder, astonishment, delight and beauty comes a nearness to God unimaginable in the swamp of disobedience and the jungle of materialism. This is not heaven but a wonderful illusion of heaven. To be truly heaven everyone now living in the swamp must be here with him.

"Oh my brother, oh my sister, my neighbor, my friend and all mankind, now living in that swamp. No! No! a thousand times no! I must go back and try to tell them about reality, I must get them here," he cries.

Forgetful of self and filled with a selfless devotion he plunges back down the river back into the jungle and back into the swamp. He rushes up to everyone he meets, pleads, begs, weeps and cries, "Please row, it's there, it's really there." He puts the paddle in their hands and directs them toward the river. He tells them about the current knowing full well they will have to find it all out for themselves. He warns them about the snags, the whirlpools, the rocks, the rapids, the waterfalls and tries inadequately to describe what he had discovered. To every willing listener he gives a guide book.

Now a very wonderful thing happens. The hand of God reaches down and lifts him into a higher level of heaven. A placeless place so wonderful it is inexplicable. Timeless, placeless and the heaven of heavens where one becomes one with the divine Manifestation of our Creator. Words have no meaning. Feelings melt into nothingness. Beauty has lost its very meaning. On every side the melody of heaven sings, "Glory, Glory, Glory be to God." The occupant and his canoe are still in the jungle and swamp but in reality they are tossed upon the sea of Glory and reunited with their Source.

If the occupant had returned down the river to obtain this higher level of heaven he would never have reached it. This can only be attained through selfless sacrifice of the other states of heaven. He would even go into the depths of hell fire for the sake of others. To reach this state of heaven one can't have even the slightest trace of self or desire. When this state is reached. "IN EVERY FACE ONE SEES THE FACE OF GOD."

> *This is the plane whereon the vestiges of all things (Kullu Shay') are destroyed in the traveler, and on the horizon of eternity the Divine Face riseth out of the darkness, and the meaning of "All on the earth shall pass away, but the face of thy Lord...." is made manifest.*

A vestige is a trace or what remains, like a foot print in the sand. Here the word used is plural meaning all visible signs are destroyed. That reminds me of a story.

A man died and was sitting in the presence of Buddha for judgement on how he had spent his life. It was like watching a video of his life. Along with the pictures there were two sets of foot prints left on the sands of time as he moved through his life. He asked His Holiness why were there two sets and the Buddha replied that he was walking with him. Always when he was having the most difficult times the footprints always changed to just one set. So the man again asked the Buddha why when he needed Him most He had left. The Buddha replied, "It was during those most difficult times that I always carried you so that is why you can only see one set of prints. They are Mine."

It seems in this valley man must even give up to God his movement and stillness. All inclusive sacrifice of oneself. Then all that will be seen in the traveler and in everything the traveler sees is only the Divine Face. To the wayfarer at this stage all that is left is God, everything else has evaporated into nothingness, including himself.

> O My friend, listen with heart and soul to the songs of the spirit, and treasure them as thine own eyes. For the heavenly wisdoms, like the clouds of spring, will not rain down on the earth of men's hearts forever; and though the grace of the All-Bounteous One is never stilled and never ceasing, yet to each time and era a portion is allotted and a bounty set apart, this in a given measure. "And no one thing is there, but with Us are its storehouses; and We send it not down but in settled measure." The cloud of the Loved One's mercy raineth only on the garden of the spirit, and bestoweth this bounty only in the season of spring. The other seasons have no share in this greatest grace, and barren lands no portion of this favor.

Bahá'u'lláh is the Nightingale of Paradise singing forth His songs of love to all mankind. As these songs are from the King and all melodies from Him, surely we should listen with all our hearts and all our souls to these sweet refrains that have descended from the realm of glory. 'Abdu'l-Bahá said, "The coming of a Manifestation of God is the season of spiritual spring." So the season of our spring was from 1844 to 1892. This was the time of plowing and planting and now we are at the very start of summer when this spirit must grow, flourish and bring forth its blossoms.

As this Book was written even beore Bahá'u'lláh declared Himself a Manifestation of God it was written during the very first days of spring for the Bahá'í revelation. During that time one could physically visit, see and hear the Báb and Bahá'u'lláh. For us that time has gone as He said it would.

> O Brother! Not every sea hath pearls; not every branch will flower, nor will the nightingale sing thereon. Then, ere the nightingale of the mystic paradise repair to the garden of God, and the rays of the heavenly morning return to the Sun of Truth—make thou an

effort, that haply in this dustheap of the mortal world thou mayest catch a fragrance from the everlasting garden, and live forever in the shadow of the peoples of this city. And when thou hast attained this highest station and come to this mightiest plane, then shalt thou gaze on the Beloved, and forget all else.

> *The Beloved shineth on gate and wall*
> *Without a veil, O men of vision.*

Here is a warning for mankind: even after seeing the most profound truth some will still choose to ignore it and turn away. He further warns us to make an effort while still living in this world to obtain the gift of everlasting life. The teaching is for each and every human being on the planet earth to individually and of their own free will to investigate and to find this truth of Bahá'u'lláh for themselves.

Now hast thou abandoned the drop of life and come to the sea of the Life-Bestower. This is the goal thou didst ask for; if it be God's will, thou wilt gain it.

In this city, even the veils of light are split asunder and vanish away. "His beauty hath no veiling save light, His face no covering save revelation." How strange that while the Beloved is visible as the sun, yet the heedless still hunt after tinsel and base metal. Yea, the intensity of His revelation hath ,covered Him, and the fullness of His shining forth hath hidden Him.

> *Even as the sun, bright hath He shined,*
> *But alas, He hath come to the town of the blind!*

The above story of the river and the total destruction of self and desire make this point to the best of my ability and understanding. The people that live in the swamp have no idea of the river or the lake and are indeed blind to it for it can only be understood by experiencing it. Let me give you an example:

Once upon a time there was a world where the night and day was divided into periods of about 1000 years. The life span of the people that lived in this world was about 100 years. About 10 generations lived in the dark and about 10 generations lived in the light.

As the sun was setting the people were advised to get their light from the keepers of the lamps. The keepers of the lamps were to be the light givers for the people until the sun returned in the far reaches of time. As generation after generation came to rely more and more on these keepers of the lamps they soon became the leaders and most prominent members of society. Their voice was the voice of law and authority.

Then a small boy tending the flocks of sheep way up high in the mountains very far off saw a faint, almost invisible ray of light. He rushed down from the mountain using his lamps and roused the population stating that the sun was coming back. This boy was interviewed by the TV networks and newspapers and 99.9% of the population had a good laugh and said that the legends of the sun were only that, just legends with no historical proof. The keepers of the lamps assured the population that there was absolutely no truth in the rambling and imaginings of a shepherd boy.

That one tenth of one percent however decided to climb to the top of the highest mountain peak and check it out. Sure enough from that high point the dawning light of day was visible to all that cared to climb. Even some few of the keepers of the lamps made the climb. The dusty history Books were in the hands of the keepers of the lamps and they were duly consulted and in their hearts they knew that the sun was going to come back. They also felt that their eminent social position and leadership was in jeopardy. So they banded together and arrested, killed and imprisoned any and all proponents of the new day that was indeed dawning. However, more and more of the enlightened people went to look and more and more people were killed and imprisoned and no one dared to oppose the keepers of the lamps as they had assumed the position of sole authority and law. Although forced to act in secret the numbers of the new day group was growing and expanding.

The keepers of the lamps then began to force the people to move underground in order to maintain their positions. By the second generation after the shepherd boy first saw the light of the sun it was now visible to all above ground. The sun was up and shone in all of its radiant splendor. The people even below ground began to feel its heat and quickening power and more and more people deserted the keepers of the lamps and went above ground.

This story is a good example, of what Bahá'u'lláh means in the above passage. He has indeed come and His light has no veils and He has shone with a radiance for all to see. Yet because of the so-called political and religious leaders He has been hidden and persecuted. Nevertheless, more and more thoughtful people have decided to investigate this Divine Light and having discovered its truth have joined the ranks of this new day.

> *In this Valley, the wayfarer leaveth behind him the stages of the "oneness of Being and Manifestation" and reacheth a oneness that is sanctified above these two stations. Ecstasy alone can encompass this theme, not utterance nor argument; and whosoever hath dwelt at this stage of the journey, or caught a breath from this garden land, knoweth whereof We speak.*

Bahá'u'lláh says here that not utterance or argument can be used, only ecstasy alone. Therefore it is impossible to comment, as a comment would be meaningless for such a station.

> *In all these journeys the traveler must stray not the breadth of a hair from the "Law," for this is indeed the secret of the "Path" and the fruit of the Tree of "Truth"; and in all these stages he must cling to the robe of obedience to the commandments, and hold fast to the cord of shunning all forbidden things, that*

> he may be nourished from the cup of the Law and informed of the mysteries of Truth.

The problems we face and I mean every problem facing our world today, can be traced back to someone somewhere having set aside the laws of God. We say that we have broken God's law. Nothing could be further from the turth. We break ourselves by disobeying the laws of God. God's laws are still as strong and unbreakable as they were before we were born and so they shall be forever. I break myself against the law and I am the one broken. Here Bahá'u'lláh says not to stray even a hair breadth from the law. There is no such thing as just a little bit of disobedience. Like I will just have a little sex outside of marriage, or I will just tell a little lie. One of the secrets for traversing and getting through The Seven Valleys is to obey with heart and soul what Bahá'u'lláh tells us to do and to not do what He tells us not to do.

> If any of the utterances of this Servant may not be comprehended, or may lead to perturbation, the same must be inquired of again, that no doubt may linger, and the meaning be clear as the Face of the Beloved One shining from the "Glorious Station".

> These journeys have no visible ending in the world of time, but the severed wayfarer—if invisible confirmation descend upon him and the Guardian of the Cause assist him—may cross these seven stages in seven steps, nay rather in seven breaths, nay rather in a single breath, if God will and desire it. And this is of "His grace on such of His servants as He pleaseth".

When Bahá'u'lláh left this world in 1892 He did not leave us with no one to answer our questions. First He gave us His son 'Abdu'l-Bahá, then the Guardian, the grandson of 'Abdu'l-Bahá, Shoghi Effendi and he was followed by the Universal House of Justice which was given this authority by Bahá'u'lláh Himself. So after reading The Seven Valleys we should consult the other Writings of

Bahá'u'lláh, 'Abdu'l-Bahá, Shoghi Effendi and then if we still have not found our answers we can ask the Universal House of Justice.

In Traveling through these seven valleys, some will take seven steps and some can go through them in seven breaths and some in a single breath. This implies, however, that whether it takes seven years or one breath we still must go through the valleys, so we should one and all ardently and sincerely pray for God's grace and help to make this journey.

> *They who soar in the heaven of singleness and reach to the sea of the Absolute, reckon this city—which is the station of life in God—as the furthermost state of mystic knowers, and the farthest homeland of the lovers. But to this evanescent One of the mystic ocean, this station is the first gate of the heart's citadel, that is, man's first entrance to the city of the heart; and the heart is endowed with four stages, which would be recounted should a kindred soul be found.*

> *When the pen set to picturing this station, It broke in pieces and the page was torn.*

Again Bahá'u'lláh refers to the abundant truths from God that lay hidden within Him. It was known that, not once but many times, Bahá'u'lláh would reveal Books and Tablets because He could not restrain the spirit moving within Him only to have them cast into the river and destroyed, explaining that mankind was not yet ready for them.

Salam!

Salam means the end and peace. Bahá'u'lláh adds the following as a postscript to "The Seven Valleys".

> *O My friend! Many a hound pursueth this gazelle of the desert of oneness; many a talon claweth at this thrush of the eternal garden. Pitiless ravens do lie in wait for this bird of the heavens of God, and the*

huntsman of envy stalketh this deer of the meadow of love.

O Shaykh! Make of thine effort a glass, perchance it may shelter this flame from the contrary winds; albeit this light doth long to be kindled in the lamp of the Lord, and to shine in the globe of the spirit. For the head raised up in the love of God will certainly fall by the sword, and the life that is kindled with longing will surely be sacrificed, and the heart which remembereth the Loved One will surely brim with blood. How well is it said:

> Live free of love, for its very peace is anguish;
> Its beginning is pain, its end is death.

Peace be upon him who followeth the Right Path!

This writing is a classical style of writing as one can see from the whole Book. Bahá'u'lláh's writings even in English are very poetic and I understand that they are even more beautiful in Arabic and Farsi (Persian).

Bahá'u'lláh says to the one reading this book, "O My friend!" This implies that we are not only His friends, but that by being His friend we are also friends of God. He then likens Himself to the Gazelle of the desert of oneness, which is a very beautiful and timid animal. The thrush is a song bird that sings and is small and defenseless, but this Thrush is the bird of the eternal garden and no ordinary bird. The ravens of mankind such as the religious and political leaders of the world are lying in wait to destroy this Thrush of heaven sent to us by our Creator. The huntsman of envy refers to some of Bahá'u'lláh's own family and some of His own followers that turned against Him because of their jealousy and envy. He again refers to Himself as the deer but again a deer of no ordinary meadow, but the meadow of love.

O Shaykh! would again be referring to the person reading this Book or to mankind in general. He asks us to put forth all our effort to protect this light of God even if we are persecuted and killed in the process. We will all live and we will all one day die and no one can escape this process. The real profit is in living and dying for a purpose which is the purpose of God.

The only one to really know what Bahá'u'lláh means in the absence of 'Abdu'l-Bahá or the Guardian is Bahá'u'lláh Himself. In the future the most learned people on the planet earth will devote their entire lives to trying to grasp a fuller understanding of His writings. Shoghi Effendi said, "We hope that these elucidations will assist the friends in understanding these relationships more clearly, but we must all remember that we stand too close to the beginnings of the System ordained by Bahá'u'lláh to be able fully to understand its potentialities or the interrelationships of its component parts."

The foregoing comments are not even a drop in the ocean of real understanding. If in some small way I have helped you, dear reader in your quest to slove the riddles of life then my work will have achieved its purpose.

www.ingramcontent.com/pod-product-compliance
Lightning Source LLC
Chambersburg PA
CBHW020916090426
42736CB00008B/665